Candymaking

Kendrick & Atkinson

HPBooks

Most HPBooks are available at special quantity discounts for bulk purchases for sales promotions, premiums, fund-raising, or educational use. Special books, or book excerpts, can also be created to fit specific needs.

For details, write: Special Markets, The Berkley Publishing Group, 375 Hudson Street, New York, New York 10014.

**HPBooks
are published by
The Berkley Publishing Group
A division of Penguin Putnam Inc.**
375 Hudson Street
New York, NY 10014
© 1987 HPBooks, Inc.
Printed in the U.S.A.
20   19   18   17   16   15   14   13   12   11   10   9

**ANOTHER BEST-SELLING VOLUME
FROM HPBooks**

Food Stylist	Mable Hoffman
Assistant	Annie Horenn
Food Stylist	
Photography	deGennaro Associates

Cover photograph: Fresh Strawberry Dips (page 142)

**Library of Congress
Cataloging-in-Publication Data**

Kendrick, Ruth A., 1945
   Candymaking.

   Includes index.
   1. Candy.   I. Atkinson, Pauline H., 1909-
II. Title
TX791.K45   1987   641.8'53   87-8640
ISBN 0-89586-307-3

Notice: The information in this book is true and complete to the best of our knowledge. All recommendations are made without guarantees on the part of the authors or the publisher. The authors and publisher disclaim all liability in connection with the use of this information.

Dedication

To my husband, Ron, and children, Jeff, Melissa and Ryan, for their patience and support during this project.

To my mother, Pauline, who instilled in me at an early age the love of cooking and the desire to experiment and improve. Without her early interest in candymaking, this book would not be possible.

—Ruth

To my late husband, Melvin S. Atkinson, who encouraged me to develop my talents and who planned and printed my first little candy book. To my children, Irene, Shirley, Wayne and Nola, who through the years have helped me in many ways, and always praised and encouraged me.

Special words of praise and dedication for my daughter Ruth, for her hard work, skills and knowledge, and special efforts in co-authoring this book.

—Pauline

Acknowledgments

We thank all our friends and relatives for their willingness to taste our experiments and offer opinions and suggestions. To those who have kindly shared their finest recipes with us, we thank them.

Our special thanks go to our cousin, Ruth Sweeten, for sharing with us her knowledge of using the electric frying pan for dipping chocolates.

Our most special thanks go to our editor and friend, Jan Thiesen, for her kind understanding of first-time authors. She spent many, many hours on this project and was always very professional and positive in her approach. We thank her and the staff of HPBooks.

Our sincere thanks also to Leslie Sinclair, who took such a special interest in the total design of our book.

We also want to thank Mable Hoffman—both for her remarkable talents as a food stylist as well as for her innate graciousness, and her assistant, Annie Horenn, for making our candies look so pretty and delicious (which they are!).

And last, but certainly not least, to our kind friends at the deGennaro Studio—Tommy, David, Stan, Dennis and Dave—who took such beautiful pictures and were so very cooperative.

Ruth   *Pauline*

We add a very special thank you to Merckens Chocolate Co., division of Nabisco, Cambridge, Massachusetts, for the chocolate products used for photography.

HOW SWEET IT IS!

Pauline H. Atkinson and Ruth A. Kendrick are a mother-daughter team who together have over 90 years of experience as candymakers.

Pauline, who is 78-years old, says she has been making candy "forever." An enthusiastic, creative and inspiring lady, this mother of five, grandmother of 20 and great-grandmother of three, leads a life that would leave many people one-third her age breathless. In addition to being a classical organist and pianist, Pauline studies oil painting, reads at least two books a week, directs tours for a prominent travel agent, attends church every Sunday and, until recently, taught a special candymaking class to standing-room-only audiences at Brigham Young University.

Ruth currently operates her own candy business and writes a column on the techniques of candymaking for a local newspaper. She has a B.S. degree in Home Economics from Brigham Young, and an M.S. in Home Economics Education from Utah State University. In addition, Ruth received the prestigious Grand Champion Candymaker award at the Utah State Fair in 1979—the only year she has entered the competition. She also teaches candy classes and has given hundreds of candymaking demonstrations. A mother of three, Ruth is a licensed private pilot and she and her husband, Ron, own their own plane.

Making candy is one of Ruth's earliest memories—and she thinks that's probably because she enjoys it so much! Based on her experience and success, she sincerely believes that "there is no better candy made anywhere.

"Candymaking is the one area in which I feel extremely confident. After many years of making candy to supplement my income, I have made every conceivable mistake. I like to think that I have learned from each one, and some of these mistakes have actually led to new recipes and techniques."

Pauline feels that "this book truly tells and shows people how to make professional-quality candy at home without special equipment or training.

"Everyone needs to feel that they excel in some way, and making fine candy gives one a sense of great achievement. The candy made from our recipes is some of the best you will ever eat."

Both Ruth and Pauline feel confident that *Candymaking* can turn anyone into a top-notch candymaker. How sweet it is—and how much sweeter life will be—with the help of this book!

On pages 8 and 9: a sampling of the ideas in this book. Top shelf: Daphne's Divinity (page 77); Lollipops (page 102); chocolate truffle (pages 46-50); Marshmallow Easter Egg (page 81); Ruth's Buttermints (page 110); molded candies (pages 133-135); Shirley's Wonderful Caramels (page 63); molded Lollipops (page 102). Lower shelf: Barks (page 143); Ruth's Pecan Brittle (page 96); foil-wrapped Marshmallow Easter Eggs (page 81); truffles (pages 46-50); Mint Sandwiches (page 143); Lollipops (page 102); and Sugared Popcorn (page 126).

CONTENTS

An Introduction to CANDYMAKING

As surprising as it is to the authors, together they have been making candy for nearly a century. Pauline started with taffy when she was in her early teens, and Ruth's first candymaking venture resulted in a memorable batch of "green something."

Both have learned a lot—and they emphasize *a lot*—along the way, through their successes and, especially, their failures. They add that some of the "goofs" have turned into some of their best recipes, and both agree that even if all seems lost, don't give up—just call it something else. This kind of creative thinking has kept many a batch of candy from being poured down the drain—and they can recall more than one batch of "fudge" that became "frosting"!

This book actually came about in a somewhat unusual way. Pauline thought it might be wise to compile some of her candy recipes and have a few copies printed up for family and friends. She called the collection "Let's Make Candy" and felt that 50 copies would be more than adequate. Her husband, who coincidentally and conveniently happened to be a printer, complied with her request. To date, the "book"—60 half-pages folded and "bound" by staples—has sold over 20,000 copies. This book, *Candymaking*, is its greatly expanded full-color successor.

Ruth and Pauline emphasize they have made every candy in the book countless times and under all kinds of conditions—in their kitchens, for demonstrations and in classes—and the recipes definitely do work.

They've found that most people in their classes are eager to understand the "why's" of making professional-quality candies at home, and they recommend that aspiring candymakers read the introduction start-to-finish: the basic principles of candymaking are contained in these pages. Chemistry and technicalities are kept to a minimum, however, as neither lady thinks it's necessary to be a food technologist to make a good batch of fudge.

Both are hopeful that this information will provide the confidence and inspiration needed to whip up a favorite candy. In fact, you probably will be quite surprised at how quickly you'll be making any kind of candy you choose, rain or shine.

And never fear. If you happen to be less than a roaring success the first time out, Ruth and Pauline humbly suggest you remember that old adage: "When all else fails, read the directions and try again." Or call it "frosting."

EQUIPMENT & COOKING UTENSILS

The recipes in this book have been developed in household kitchens with normal kitchen equipment. Chances are, most of the equipment needed to make good candies is already in your kitchen.

Saucepans—For fondants, fudges and caramels you need a heavy-gauge aluminum, steel or copper saucepan. The bottom of a pressure cooker works very well. A one-handled pot is a little easier to work with because it requires only one hand to pour. A 4-quart capacity will handle most recipes in this book. For candies that don't contain cream, milk or chocolate, a lighter-weight saucepan will work. The heavier weight helps keep candies from scorching.

Cooling Pan—Glass or metal oblong cake pans measuring 9″ x 13″ or larger are used for cooling fondants, and also for melting chocolate in the oven. An 8- or 9-inch square baking pan is used for caramels, fudges and truffles. Jellyroll pans are used for caramel-nougat pinwheels, pecan rolls and caramel clusters (method 1).

Electric Frying Pan—A heavy, cast aluminum electric frying pan is best, but stainless steel will work if you keep in mind that it holds the heat longer than aluminum. The electric frying pan is used to make toffee and to control the temperature of chocolate while dipping.

Electric Mixer—Typical kitchen mixers, either portable or on a stand, are used for beating egg whites and truffles; divinity can be beaten by hand or with a heavy-duty mixer.

Boards or Trays—Wooden boards, metal trays or baking sheets covered with waxed paper are needed for the placing of chocolate centers and for the finished chocolates.

Spatulas, Scrapers & Knives—A long metal spatula is ideal for lifting cooling candies from the cooling surface. A normal assortment of rubber scrapers, pancake turners and knives is used. Wide-bladed putty knives found in hardware stores are useful for scraping chocolate and fondant.

Scissors—Household or kitchen scissors are indispensable for cutting butter mints and taffy.

Pastry Brush—A pastry brush is useful for washing down the sides of the cooking pan to make sure all sugar granules are dissolved.

Wooden Spoons and Paddles—Wooden spoons are very helpful in candymaking. Since the handles don't get hot, they are more comfortable in your hand. Also, you can detect undissolved sugar granules by feel and sound with a wooden spoon. A wooden spoon or paddle is necessary for stirring fondants and fudges; a metal spoon can bend or make blisters on your hand.

After stirring a sugar mixture, be sure that the spoon is thoroughly rinsed before returning it to the pan for any additional stirring. Even a single sugar granule remaining on the spoon can cause a chain reaction and the entire batch of candy can develop a grainy texture.

Marble Slab—Many people think that you can't make candy without a marble slab—but you certainly can! Marble is desirable because it stays cold, which allows fondants to cool quickly without movement; with a few precautions, though, a 9″ x 13″ or slightly larger pan substitutes well.

Marble is admittedly very useful in making pulled buttermints and taffy but, here again, we have found that a chilled jellyroll pan can be used instead. However, if you do make a lot of these candies, you may find it helpful to invest in this particular piece of equipment.

Marble is also used for dipping chocolates, but we would like to add that it takes a lot of practice to develop the technique of using marble for this purpose. The electric frying pan method is much easier to learn and we recommend it instead, especially for the beginner or for people who will only occasionally be dipping chocolates.

Confectioner suppliers carry an assortment of marble slabs, which are available in several sizes—18-inch square is the most common. A plastic countertop is not a good substitute; it does not retain the cold like marble, and you could damage the surface.

For accuracy, it is important to read candy thermometer at eye level.

COLD WATER TEST

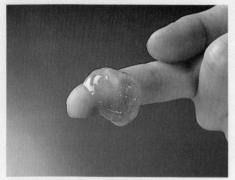

Soft ball: 234-240F (110-115C)

Firm ball: 242-248F (115-120C)

Dipping Fork—Dipping forks are used if you do not wish to dip with your hands, and for dipping maraschino cherries in melted fondant. They can be purchased from confectioner suppliers, or a regular table fork can be used as a substitute. A fondue fork, slightly bent or curved with pliers—use a gentle touch—also works well.

Molds—Metal molds or specially treated plastic molds can be purchased at many specialty shops. They are used for hot syrups such as for lollipops and hard candies. This syrup is very hot and would melt normal molds used for chocolate. Plastic molds are used for chocolate molding as well as for compound or confectioners coatings. Keep these free of scratches: the shinier the surface, the shinier the finished candies will be.

Thermometers—A good candy thermometer is not absolutely necessary, but it is very useful. In selecting a candy thermometer, look for one that has two-degree markings (5-degree markings are not accurate enough for candymaking), a stainless steel back, and a clip to attach to the cooking pan. Thermometers should be handled carefully, not bumped, and stored in a safe place. With such care, a good thermometer should last you for many years.

What a thermometer tells you is how much water has boiled out in the form of steam. If you boil plain water, it will not increase in temperature above the boiling point. When a sugar solution is boiled, the temperature will rise as the water is boiled out and the sugar solution concentrates.

A thermometer needs to be tested before its initial use, and occasionally thereafter. To do this, place the thermometer in a pan with enough water to cover the bulb. Bring the water to a boil and let the water boil for several minutes. Read the temperature at eye level; if you look down, the temperature will appear to be lower than it actually is. Note the temperature at which the water boils. It will probably be between 200-212F (95-100C).

There are two factors which cause a variation in the reading. First, each thermometer is slightly different, even the same brand; and second, temperature is affected by your altitude above sea level. Water boils at about 212F at sea level and decreases approximately two degrees Fahrenheit for each 1000 feet rise in altitude. Thus, if you live at 4000 feet, water will boil at about 204F (95C). This is due to the difference in air pressure.

Remember, in candymaking the thermometer tells you how much water has boiled out of the sugar solution. If water boils at a lower temperature, which it does at higher altitudes, the water is boiling out at a lower temperature. This means that your candy will actually reach the properly cooked stage at a lower temperature.

Almost all candy recipes, including those in this book, are written for sea level and must be adjusted for your altitude. Regardless of the altitude at which you live, test your thermometer in boiling water and write down the boiling point. If it boils at any temperature other than 212F (100C), adjust the temperature according to the chart on the following page.

Even though we have included both Celsius and Fahrenheit readings, we urge you to use a Fahrenheit thermometer; the wide range between degrees on the Celsius scale is not accurate enough for candymaking.

You have probably heard that you shouldn't make candy when it rains or snows. This is not factual. You can make candy very successfully during wet weather. It isn't the humidity that causes problems, but the changes in air pressure. If you question the weather, simply retest your thermometer and adjust according to the chart.

Your thermometer will fluctuate with the weather. Retest occasionally and adjust recipes when necessary. If it is very humid, be sure to store your candies in airtight containers to keep out the moisture.

COLD WATER TEST FOR SYRUPS

If you don't have access to a thermometer, rely on the cold-water test. The procedure is as follows:

Place a small amount of syrup to be tested in a cup of very cold water. If the syrup forms a soft ball in the water but flattens when removed, it is at the soft-ball stage—234-240F (110-115C).

The firm ball stage has been reached when the syrup dropped into cold water forms a firm ball which does not flatten when removed from the water—242-248F (115-120C).

The hard ball stage is reached when the syrup forms a hard but still pliable ball when removed from the water—250-268F (120-130C).

Soft crack occurs when the syrup separates into threads which are hard but not brittle—270-290F (130-145C).

Hard crack stage is reached when the syrup separates into threads which are hard and brittle—300-310F (150-155C).

The problem with this method of testing is that by the time you decide the candy has cooked enough, it has probably increased several degrees. The markings on the thermometer for soft ball, hard ball, etc. should be ignored unless your thermometer boils at 212F (100C).

Hard ball: 250-268F (120-130C)

Soft crack: 270-290F (130-145C)

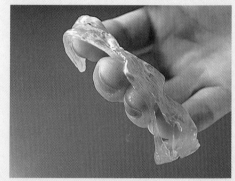
Hard crack: 300-310F (150-155C)

If the water boils when the thermometer reaches	200F (93C)	Subtract	12F (7C)	from recipe
"	201F (94C)	"	11F (6C)	"
"	202F (94C)	"	10F (6C)	"
"	203F (95C)	"	9F (5C)	"
"	204F (95C)	"	8F (5C)	"
"	205F (96C)	"	7F (4C)	"
"	206F (96C)	"	6F (4C)	"
"	207F (97C)	"	5F (3C)	"
"	208F (98C)	"	4F (2C)	"
"	209F (98C)	"	3F (2C)	"
"	210F (99C)	"	2F (1C)	"
"	211F (99C)	"	1F (1C)	"
"	212F (100C)	"	0F (0C)	"

For example, when testing your thermometer, if the water boils at 204F and the recipe calls for cooking to 238F, subtract 8 degrees and cook to 230F. Most recipes have a 1 to 2 degree cushion built into them, but try to be as accurate as you possibly can.

INGREDIENTS

Solid Sugars

Granulated sugar is white table sugar, either cane or beet. Some candymakers prefer cane sugar as it doesn't foam as much, but there is little if any difference in the finished candy.

Brown sugar is less refined than granulated sugar and contains a small amount of molasses. Both light brown and dark brown are available and it is a matter of personal preference which kind you use. We prefer the light brown because it gives a more delicate flavor. When measuring brown sugar, pack it firmly in the measuring cup and level it off with a knife or metal spatula.

The acid found in brown sugars sometimes causes the milk to curdle when these two ingredients are cooked together. If this occurs, add a pinch of baking soda to the mixture as it boils and curdling will be reduced.

Powdered sugar—which is also called confectioners sugar—is a very finely milled sugar that has cornstarch added to it.

Liquid Sugars

Corn syrup is used to control the amount of graining. Our recipes have been developed using corn syrup readily available at supermarkets. Usually we use light corn syrup, but occasionally a recipe refers to dark corn syrup. This product is less refined and, like dark brown sugar, gives a stronger, more pronounced flavor to your candy.

If too much corn syrup is used in soft candies, such as fondants, they will take a long time to set up and won't be as tender as they should be. With caramels, too much corn syrup causes a tough, chewy product. In hard candies it is necessary to control the graining tendency of sugar. If too much corn syrup is used in hard candies, it will cause them to be sticky.

Molasses is used in a few of our recipes where a pronounced flavor is desired. Either light or dark may be used and, again, the lighter product gives a more delicate flavor.

Honey is an invert sugar that causes a softening action to take place in the finished candies. A light, mild honey is recommended as the flavor of the honey is left in the candy.

Typical ingredients and supplies used in candymaking.

1. Milk chocolate, 2. White chocolate, 3. Semisweet chocolate, 4. Wooden spoon, 5. Candy thermometer, 6. Corn syrup, 7. Milk, 8. Granulated sugar, 9. Red and green candied cherries, 10. Compound coatings, 11. Paper cups, 12. Macadamia nuts, 13. Raw peanuts, 14. Butter, 15. Pecans and walnuts, 16. Plastic molds and 17. Pastry brush

Milk Products

Whipping cream, which has a butterfat content between 35-40%, is used in many of our recipes. It adds flavor, fat and milk solids. Do not substitute evaporated milk for the cream.

Milk is usually used with whipping cream to add more milk solids. Use fresh fluid milk, either skim, 1%, low-fat or whole. When using the lower fat milks, your candy may not be as rich.

Evaporated milk provides extra milk solids, which makes caramels have more body. It also has a "cooked" taste, which is covered up in caramels but may be objectionable in other candies. Don't use evaporated milk unless it is specifically called for in a recipe. When evaporated milk is used, be sure to stir continually as it will scorch easily.

Sweetened condensed milk is whole milk which has sugar added and the amount of water reduced. There is no satisfactory substitute for this milk.

Fats

Butter is preferred over margarine in our recipes. The flavor is far superior to margarine, and the cost difference is not that great. Don't substitute margarine for butter unless the recipe gives that alternative. When margarine is used, be sure to buy high-quality, vegetable oil margarines.

Chocolate

Baking chocolate—also known as chocolate liquor—is pure chocolate with no sugar added. It is very strong, very bitter and contains a high cocoa butter content that causes the fat to come to the surface when stored at too high a temperature. This is called "bloom" and will not affect the quality of the chocolate; once it is heated, the fat returns in suspension.

Baking chocolate is used to flavor fondants and caramels, and any other candy when a pronounced chocolate flavor is desired.

Unsweetened cocoa is similar to baking chocolate except it has less cocoa butter and is finely ground.

If you need to substitute unsweetened cocoa for baking chocolate (or vice-versa), use this equation:

1 square (1-ounce) baking chocolate = 3 tablespoons unsweetened cocoa plus 1 tablespoon butter or margarine.

Dipping chocolate is made by a complex process. Emulsifiers are added to the chocolate liquor to keep the fats in suspension, as is sugar and additional cocoa butter. Milk chocolate has milk solids added to give a mild flavor.

There is no substitute for quality dipping chocolate. If it is not available in your area, check the supplier list on page 155.

Other Ingredients

Compound or confectionery coatings are available under a variety of different names. Some of the most common are almond bark, molding chocolate, summer coating, bon bon coating, Rainbow Wafers, Smooth-'n-Melty, Pastels, white chocolate (a misnomer) and Ice Caps. They are made from a vegetable oil base rather than cocoa butter, and contain sugar, milk solids, flavoring and coloring.

Coatings are used both for molding candies and as an ingredient in some of our recipes. They are not as high in quality as dipping chocolate, but they are easier to work with. Many shapes, colors and flavors are available and it is important to know what you are buying; for example, green could be vanilla-, lime-, or mint-flavored. They are a good choice for summer, or hot weather dipping, as they will set up more readily than dipping chocolate.

Compound coatings have a waxy feel when eaten due to the vegetable oil base. Never add paraffin or any other substance to your chocolate or coatings.

Marshmallow creme or mazetta—when a recipe calls for mazetta, you can make your own from our recipe on page 82, or you can purchase marshmallow creme at the supermarket. It adds a light, fluffy texture to your fondants, and though it isn't necessary to use it—you will notice it is optional in some of our recipes—it will make your candy extra-special.

Mazetta can be made ahead and stored in the refrigerator several weeks or, again, commercial marshmallow creme is a very acceptable substitute.

Cream of tartar, in very small amounts, is used to chemically change a sugar mixture. Without getting too technical, this ingredient adds an acid that rearranges the molecules—which ends up softening the candy. Cream of tartar is often added in place of corn syrup to control graining in some fondant recipes.

Citric acid is used for flavoring fruits, and to cause fondants to mellow and become smoother. Dry or liquid forms are available and either one can be used in our recipes. It can be purchased from some pharmacies, or check our supplier list on page 155.

Paste food colors are most commonly used by cake decorators because they give intense color without adding liquid. They are available wherever cake decorating supplies are sold, or from our supplier list on page 155.

Flavorings as either extracts or oil flavoring can be used in our recipes. Extracts are commonly found in supermarkets. Oils are available at some supermarkets, pharmacies and confectioner suppliers, or check the list on page 155.

Flavoring is largely a matter of personal taste: some people like a stronger flavor and others prefer a more delicate touch. Start with a little and add to taste. Remember that oils are at least twice as strong as extracts so use accordingly. Oil flavorings are necessary for hard candies as the liquid added in extracts causes too much steam in the hard candies. Flavorings weaken with age so it's best to purchase them in small quantities.

Salt is used in most of our recipes for two reasons: it enhances other flavors and cuts the too-sweet taste of some candies. This ingredient is not necessary for anything other than flavor, so if you are restricting your salt intake, you can safely leave it out.

Nuts should always be fresh. Keep nut meats in the refrigerator or freezer until ready to use. Due to their high fat content nuts can quickly turn rancid. Some of the more popular varieties are pecans, peanuts, walnuts, cashews, Brazils, filberts and macadamias.

Nuts can easily be roasted or toasted at home. Simply arrange them in a single layer on a baking sheet and place them in a preheated 300F (150C) oven for 15 minutes. Stir and taste, taking care not to burn your mouth. If they are not toasted enough, leave them in a little longer, tasting every 2 to 3 minutes until the desired flavor is reached.

RECOOKING CANDIES

Fondants, fudges and caramels can be recooked if they are under- or overcooked or if the candy "sugars," as long as the candy has not been scorched. It's a simple procedure and can save your batch. This is what you do:

In a heavy saucepan, combine 1-1/2 cups water and the cooked candy. Place over low heat and stir with a wooden spoon until the mixture is well-blended. Increase the heat to medium and bring to a boil. If sugar crystals are present, wash down the sides of the pan with a wet pastry brush. Clip on a candy thermometer and cook to the proper temperature. Pour out and cool according to the original recipe. As the old flavoring will have cooked out, be sure to add more. Your candy will have a darker color due to the increased caramelization of the sugar during the longer cooking time.

FIX-UPS

Divinity cannot be recooked, but if it is undercooked and won't hold its shape, stir in 1/4 cup powdered sugar with a wooden spoon. Allow the candy to stand 5 to 10 minutes—or until it holds its shape when spooned out.

If divinity is overcooked and too stiff when spooned out, stir in hot water 1 tablespoon at a time. Mix with a wooden spoon until soft peaks form as candy is dropped from a spoon.

If fondant is too soft, knead in macaroon or flake coconut and allow it to stand 10 minutes so the coconut can absorb the excess moisture. Proceed with shaping into centers according to recipe.

If fondant is too firm, wrap it in plastic wrap and cover with a warm tea towel for 15 minutes. Knead with your hands just as you would for bread dough. If the fondant is still too stiff, knead in 3 tablespoons of softened butter.

SWEET SUGGESTIONS
FOR HOLIDAYS AND SPECIAL OCCASIONS

Valentine's Day
Daphne's Divinity (colored pink), page 77
Popcorn Cake, page 127
Molded candies, pages 133-135
Sugared Popcorn (colored pink), page 126
Cherry Cordials, pages 86-88

Easter
Divinity Eggs, page 77
Marshmallow Easter Eggs, page 81
Molded candies, pages 133-135
Assorted dipped chocolates
Easter Nests, page 135

Mother's Day
Her favorite candy
Assorted dipped chocolates
Pecan Rolls, page 69 *or* Pecan Logs, page 70
Caramel-Nougat Pinwheels, page 80
Quick Penouche, page 51

Father's Day
His favorite candy
Caramel Clusters, page 70
Fudge, pages 51-58, 114-115
Ruth's Pecan Brittle, page 96

4th of July
Popcorn Cake (with flags), page 127
Fudgels, pages 115-120

Halloween
Molded candies in black, orange and white,
pages 133-135
Tender Marshmallows (flavored
with orange extract), page 81
Quick Peanut Butter Treats, page 131
Caramel Apples, page 70
Chocolate Caramels, page 68

Thanksgiving
Marzipan fruits (in a cornucopia), pages 136-141
Caramel Corn, page 73
Ruth's Buttermints, page 110
Ruth's Pecan Brittle, page 96
Sour Cream Nuts, page 122

Christmas
Assorted dipped chocolates
Caramels, pages 61-68
Caramel-Nougat Pinwheels, page 80
Fudgels, pages 115-120
Nougats, pages 79-80
Christmas Walnuts, page 123
Pauline's Peanut Brittle, page 97
Holiday Fudge, page 52
Amy's Toffee, page 105
Marzipan decorations, pages 136-141

Child's Birthday
Sugared Popcorn (multi-colored), page 126
Popcorn Cake (with balloons), page 127
Lollipops, page 102
Molded candies, pages 133-135
Baked Caramel Corn, page 72
An old-fashioned taffy pull, pages 106-109

Adult's Birthday
Find out what their favorite candy is
and make them a batch or two

Weddings
Ruth's Buttermints, page 110
Molded candies, pages 133-135
Mint Sandwiches, page 143
Candied nuts, pages 100-101, 122-123
Fudgels, pages 115-120
Maggie's No-Fail Chocolate Fudge, page 55

Present your homemade candies in fresh new ways: A see-through plastic box shows off a combination of Pauline's Peanut Brittle (page 97) and Coconut-Cashew Brittle (page 98); your sweetheart will enjoy nibbling from a pretty arrangement of heart-shaped molded candies (pages 133-135), displayed in a contemporary, heart-shaped candy dish; and a "bouquet" of assorted dipped chocolates (throughout book) tied, literally, with a necktie, makes an irresistible—and memorable—gift idea for Father's Day.

STORAGE CONTAINERS

Shoe boxes with lids, metal tins, or plastic ware are some of the containers that can be used to store candies. Some candies must be stored airtight, and this information will be included with the recipe.

SHIPPING

Many candies ship well, particularly in the cooler months. Heavy candies such as fudges, caramels, nougats and hard candies ship better than brittles, truffles or jellies; divinity that is spread into a pan instead of being spooned out onto waxed paper ships quite satisfactorily. Chocolates do well if they are insulated with several layers of newspaper. Cherry cordials are an exception as they are delicate and tend to crush in shipping.

Choose a firm container, such as a metal tin, shoe box with lid, plastic ware, or well-washed and aired coffee tins. Place the candy in plastic bags, wrap it in foil, or place it in smaller containers. Pack the container firmly with the candy and place several layers of paper toweling directly on top of the candy to act as a cushion. Tape or seal the container and place it in a cardboard box. Pack the edges, bottom and top with crumpled newspaper, plastic foam pellets or unbuttered, unsalted popped corn. Seal the container and mark it "perishable."

Candies will absorb moisture and be affected by heat, so plan your shipping times according to the weather at the destination as well as departure point.

A trio of fondants: the magical Cherry
Cordial (pages 86-88); a chocolate-
dipped fondant rolled in chopped nuts
(use any of the fondant recipes); and
Apricot Cream Fondant (page 31)
dipped in melted compound coating
(pages 134, 146-153).

Fondants

If you want to become a first-class candymaker, learning to make smooth, creamy fondant is a must. Fondants are the basis for many candies—chocolate centers, pecan log centers and fruit cordials, to name a few. With a minimal number of basic fondant recipes, you can make an endless variety of candies, simply by varying the flavoring and adding fruits or nuts.

Have you ever wondered how the liquid gets inside a cherry cordial? The "liquid" is actually fondant—and the fondant is firm when it is wrapped around the cherry. The cherry juice acting on the sugar in the fondant causes it to liquefy days later—*after* being encased in chocolate.

Most of our fondant recipes require hand-stirring, which can be strenuous, but with the concern for physical fitness today, consider it part of your exercise routine.

Unless specified, our fondant recipes do not need to "age" or ripen; they are ready to dip the day they are made. Fondants can also be made ahead and stored in airtight containers or bags in the refrigerator or the freezer. They will keep several weeks in the refrigerator and three to four months in the freezer. Freezing tends to make the fondant smoother and softer due to a chemical change that takes place. Occasionally, however, they will become slightly sticky and hard to handle. If this happens, use cornstarch on your hands to work with the fondant.

Fondants have few ingredients. Basically, they consist of sugar, corn syrup or cream of tartar, cream or milk, water and salt. It is the proportion of these ingredients and the length of time they are cooked that determines the final characteristics of the candy.

MAKING FONDANT

Cooked fondant is poured quickly, without scraping, into a baking pan and allowed to cool until bottom of pan is no longer warm.

Cooled fondant is stirred with a wooden paddle or spoon. Initial stirring requires minimal effort—just enough motion to keep the fondant moving.

Fondant develops a creamier texture about half-way through stirring. At this point, it may be easier to use both hands on the paddle for the remainder of the stirring.

Always use a heavy saucepan when making fondant. As we mentioned in our introduction, we find that the bottom of a pressure cooker works very well. Again, as with all candies, place the liquids in the pan first, then the sugar. This will help eliminate sugar crystals on the sides of the cooking pan.

If any sugar crystals do stick to the edge, wash down the sides of the pan with a wet pastry brush or a damp paper towel. Do be very careful if using the paper towel method because it's easy to get burned by the steam. You can also cover the pan with a lid for about one minute. Condensation created by the trapped steam will run down the sides of the pan and dissolve the crystals. The caution with this method is not to get busy doing something else and leave the lid on too long—and overcook the syrup in the process. (We really prefer the pastry brush method.)

Cook the fondant uncovered to the specified temperature. Immediately pour it into the cooling pan *without scraping*. Cool the fondant as rapidly as possible, either in the refrigerator or outside if it is a cool day. Do not cool the candy in the freezer.

When the bottom of the pan is no longer warm, begin stirring with a wooden spoon or paddle. You don't have to stir fast, just keep the mass moving. If you cooled your fondant too long and it is hard to stir, place it in a warm oven for a few minutes *just* until it softens slightly and is easier to stir. The warmer the fondant is when you begin to stir it, the grainier the finished product will be. If you want a smooth, creamy fondant, you must wait until all the heat is out before you begin stirring.

If you are going to make the entire batch one flavor, you can flavor it anytime during the stirring process. If you wish, you may also add mazetta (page 82) or marshmallow creme during the stirring to make the fondant lighter and fluffier. You can purchase marshmallow creme at the supermarket, or make your own mazetta. We prefer our recipe as we find it is easier to work with, more tender—and less expensive.

Stir the fondant until it loses its shine and begins to set up. It resembles thick frosting at this point. It sometimes sets up in as little as 15 minutes, but generally takes 30 to 40 minutes of stirring. If, after stirring, it hardens too much, wrap the fondant in plastic wrap and cover it with a warm damp tea towel for 15 minutes. This should cause it to soften. Sometimes you may find that lumps form in the fondant and you have to knead it like bread dough. If the fondant won't soften, you probably overcooked it. Follow the directions on page 17 for recooking.

If you have stirred the fondant for more than 1 hour and it hasn't set up, try letting it rest for a few minutes without stirring. This will sometimes cause the fondant to begin the desired crystallization process. If resting the fondant doesn't work, it may be undercooked. Follow directions for recooking on page 17.

If you are going to make several flavors out of one batch, stir without adding any flavoring.

When the batch has set up, separate it into 2 to 3 balls. Flavor each one separately, working the flavors and colors in with your hands. You will probably find this to be somewhat of a sticky process.

Be sure and wash your hands thoroughly between each flavor change. Some flavors are very strong and, once on your hands, could transfer to another portion of fondant.

Citric acid is used in fruit creams to bring out the fruit flavors and add a touch of tartness. It is available at many pharmacies, or consult the supplier list on page 155. Use either liquid or dry citric acid; the amount and the results are the same.

Once your fondant is set up and flavored, you are ready to store it or dip it. If you are going to store it, wrap it airtight in plastic wrap and place it in the refrigerator or freezer. If you are going to use it immediately, the next step is to form the fondant into the desired shapes.

SHAPING FONDANT FOR CENTERS

For chocolate centers—fondant that will be dipped in tempered chocolate or melted compound coating—pinch off a piece of fondant about the size of a large golf ball. Roll it out into a rope-shape about 1/2 inch thick. Using a table knife, cut the fondant in sections approximately 1 inch long. Next, roll each section in the palms of your hands to resemble a small ball. Place these balls on a waxed paper-lined tray.

If the fondant is too sticky to work with comfortably, wash and dry your hands thoroughly and dust them with cornstarch or flour. Powdered sugar will only make the fondant stickier. Continue with the remaining fondant until the entire batch is shaped.

With your finger tips, slightly flatten the balls of fondant on the trays. This will make them look more professional when they are dipped in chocolate or coating.

Stir the fondant until it loses its shine and reaches the consistency of thick frosting, which takes from 15 to 40 minutes.

To shape fondant into centers: roll a portion of the fondant into a rope-shape about 1/2 inch thick. Cut it into pieces about 1 inch long using a table knife or spatula.

The fondant pieces are rolled into balls, arranged on a tray, and flattened slightly with finger tips, which gives a professional look to the finished chocolates. The fondant is now ready for dipping in tempered chocolate or melted compound coating.

Cream Fondant

Use this basic recipe to make a variety of flavored centers for dipped chocolates.

1 cup whipping cream	1/4 teaspoon salt
1/2 cup milk	1/2 cup Mazetta (page 82) or
1/3 cup light corn syrup	marshmallow creme, if desired
4 cups sugar	Flavoring and/or nuts, if desired

Set aside a 9" x 13" ungreased baking pan. In a heavy 4-quart saucepan, combine cream, milk, corn syrup, sugar and salt. Place over medium-high heat and stir occasionally with a wooden spoon until mixture comes to a boil. If any sugar crystals are present, wash down sides of pan with a wet pastry brush.

Clip on candy thermometer. Cook syrup to 238F (115C) or soft-ball stage. Remove from heat and, without stirring or scraping, pour into baking pan. Without excess movement, place in refrigerator or other cool area.

When bottom of pan no longer feels warm, begin stirring fondant with a wooden spoon. You don't have to stir rapidly, just keep the mass moving. If desired, after 15 minutes of stirring add 1/2 cup mazetta or marshmallow creme. If you intend to flavor the entire batch one flavor (variations follow), you can add the flavoring and/or nuts anytime after the mazetta is added. Stir until fondant becomes very stiff and loses its gloss. At this point it has set up.

If it is too stiff to handle, break off small pieces and work them in your hands like modeling clay. This should cause it to soften. You could also wrap the fondant in plastic wrap and cover it with a warm damp tea towel for 15 minutes. This will also cause it to soften. If it doesn't, it may be overcooked. Follow directions for recooking fondant on page 17.

If you have stirred the fondant for more than 1 hour and it hasn't set up, try letting it rest for a few minutes without stirring. This will sometimes cause the fondant to begin the desired crystallization process. If resting the fondant doesn't work, it may be undercooked. Follow directions for recooking on page 17.

Cream Fondant Flavor Variations
The following variations are based on flavoring an entire batch one flavor. If you are dividing it into several different flavors, reduce the amounts of flavorings accordingly.

For Vanilla or Vanilla Nut—Add 1 tablespoon vanilla and 1 cup chopped pecans or walnuts.

For Black Walnut—Add 1 tablespoon vanilla, 1/4 teaspoon black walnut extract and 1 cup walnuts.

For Cherry Creams—Flavor with 2 teaspoons almond extract and 1 teaspoon rum extract.

For Cherry Nut—Add 2 teaspoons almond extract, 1 teaspoon rum extract, 1/2 cup chopped candied cherries and 1 cup chopped pecans, walnuts or almonds.

For Mint Creams—Add 1/2 teaspoon oil of peppermint or 2 teaspoons peppermint extract.

For Lemon Creams—Add 1 tablespoon lemon extract, a small amount of yellow food color and 1/4 teaspoon citric acid.

For Orange Creams—Add 1 tablespoon orange extract, a small amount of orange food color and 1/4 teaspoon citric acid.

For Raspberry or Strawberry Creams—Add 2 tablespoons raspberry or strawberry extract, 1/4 teaspoon lemon extract, a small amount of pink or red food color and 1/4 teaspoon citric acid.

Making several flavors from one batch

After Cream Fondant has set up, divide it into 2 or 3 balls. Press your thumb into the center of one of the portions of fondant, creating a small hole. Pour desired flavoring and color into hole and knead with your hands until well-mixed. You may also work in nuts at this time.

Sometimes the fondant becomes too sticky to handle. If it does, wash your hands and dry them thoroughly. Dust your hands with cornstarch or flour; powdered sugar makes fondant stickier.

Shaping fondants into centers

When fondant is flavored and set up, it is ready for forming into centers for chocolates, or for storage. Cover 2 trays or baking sheets with waxed paper; set aside. To shape fondant for centers, break off approximately 1/2 cup of fondant. Roll the fondant into a rope 1/2 inch thick. With a table knife, cut into 1-inch pieces.

Place the pieces one at a time in the palms of your hands and roll into balls. Arrange the balls on the waxed paper-lined trays. Continue until all fondant is rolled out. With your finger tips, slightly flatten each ball. This will give a more professional look to the finished chocolates.

The fondant centers are ready to dip immediately, or could stand at room temperature overnight, if desired. If your fondant is very soft, let the centers stand for several hours to form a crust before dipping. To dip, see information in the Chocolate chapter (beginning on page 146).

If you are going to store fondant, wrap it in plastic wrap or place it in a plastic bag. Fondant can be stored in the refrigerator for several weeks or frozen for several months. Allow it to warm to room temperature before unwrapping. Proceed as directed above for shaping the centers. Makes about 100 centers.

For Neapolitans—Divide one batch of Cream Fondant into 3 equal-sized balls. Add vanilla to one; flavor one strawberry and color it pink; and make one chocolate by kneading in 3 tablespoons unsweetened cocoa.

On a counter top, flatten each fondant into a 4-inch square. Place the vanilla fondant on top of the strawberry fondant, and cover the vanilla fondant with the chocolate fondant. You now have a 3-layer square of fondant. Cut into 1/2-inch wide strips, then cut each strip into 1-inch pieces. Roll each piece into a smooth ball. Proceed with dipping, following instructions in the Chocolate chapter (beginning on page 146).

Water Fondant

Very good for mints or fruit centers—and this fondant actually improves with age.

1-1/3 cups water
1/3 cup light corn syrup
1/4 cup butter
4 cups sugar
1/4 teaspoon cream of tartar

1/8 teaspoon salt
1 cup Mazetta (page 82) or
    marshmallow creme, if desired
Flavoring and food color
    (variations follow)

Set aside a 9'' x 13'' ungreased baking pan. In a heavy 4-quart saucepan, combine water, corn syrup, butter, sugar, cream of tartar and salt. Place over high heat and bring to a boil, stirring occasionally with a wooden spoon. When syrup reaches a boil, wash down sides of pan with a wet pastry brush; this fondant will grain easily if any sugar remains undissolved.

Clip on candy thermometer. Cook without stirring to 240F (115C) or soft-ball stage. Remove from heat and, without stirring or scraping, pour into baking pan. Without excess movement, place in refrigerator or other cool area.

When bottom of pan no longer feels warm, begin stirring fondant with a wooden spoon. If desired, stir in mazetta or marshmallow creme. Add flavoring and color. Stir the fondant until it loses its shine and begins to set up. It resembles thick frosting at this point. It sometimes sets up in as little as 15 minutes, but generally takes 30 to 40 minutes of stirring.

If, after stirring, it hardens too much, wrap the fondant in plastic wrap and cover it with a warm damp tea towel for 15 minutes. This should cause it to soften. Sometimes you may find that lumps form in the fondant and you have to knead it like bread dough. If the fondant won't soften, you probably overcooked it. Follow the directions on page 17 for recooking.

If you have stirred the fondant for more than 1 hour and it hasn't set up, try letting it rest for a few minutes without stirring. This will sometimes cause the fondant to begin the desired crystallization process. If resting the fondant doesn't work, it may be undercooked. Follow directions for recooking on page 17.

Water Fondant Flavor Variations
For Mint Creams—Add 1/4 teaspoon oil of peppermint and 6 drops green food color.
For Orange Creams—Add 1-1/2 teaspoons orange extract, 1/4 teaspoon citric acid and 4 drops orange food color.
For Raspberry Creams—Add 1-1/2 teaspoons raspberry extract, 1/4 teaspoon lemon extract and 4 drops red food color.
For Coconut Creams—Add 1 cup flaked coconut along with 1-1/2 teaspoons vanilla or coconut extract.

Making several flavors from one batch

After Water Fondant has set up, divide it into 2 or 3 balls. Press your thumb into the center of one of the portions, creating a small hole. Pour desired flavoring and color into hole and knead with your hands until it is well-mixed. You may also work in nuts at this time.

Sometimes the fondant becomes too sticky to handle. If this happens, wash hands and dry them thoroughly. Dust hands with cornstarch or flour; powdered sugar makes fondant stickier.

Shaping fondant into centers

When fondant is flavored and set up, it is ready for forming into centers for chocolates, or for storage. Cover 2 trays or baking sheets with waxed paper; set aside. To shape fondant for centers, break off approximately 1/2 cup of fondant. Roll the fondant into a rope 1/2 inch thick. With a table knife, cut the candy into pieces 1 inch long.

Place the pieces one at a time in the palms of your hands and roll into balls. Arrange the balls on the waxed paper-lined trays. Continue until all fondant is rolled out. With your finger tips, slightly flatten each ball. This will give a more professional look to the finished chocolates.

The fondant centers are ready to dip immediately or they can stand at room temperature overnight, if desired. If your fondant is very soft, let the centers stand for several hours to form a crust before dipping. To dip, see information in the Chocolate chapter (beginning on page 146).

If you are going to store fondant, wrap it in plastic wrap or place it in a plastic bag. Fondant can be stored in the refrigerator for several weeks or frozen for several months. Allow it to warm to room temperature before unwrapping. Proceed as described in the instructions above for shaping the centers. Makes about 100 centers.

Honey Buttercream Fondant

These light, fluffy chocolate centers improve with age. This is a basic recipe that can be used with many flavor variations.

1-1/3 cups whipping cream
2/3 cup milk
1/4 cup mild, light honey
2 tablespoons butter

4 cups sugar
1/2 cup Mazetta (page 82) or
    marshmallow creme
Flavorings and/or nuts (variations follow)

Set aside a 9″ x 13″ ungreased baking pan. In a heavy 4-quart saucepan, combine cream, milk, honey, butter and sugar. Place over high heat and stir constantly until mixture comes to a boil. If sugar crystals are present, wash down sides of pan with a wet pastry brush.

Clip on candy thermometer. Cook, stirring occasionally, to 240F (115C) or soft-ball stage. Remove from heat and, without stirring or scraping, pour into baking pan. Without excess movement, place in refrigerator or other cool area.

When bottom of pan no longer feels warm, begin stirring fondant with a wooden spoon. You don't have to stir rapidly, just keep the mass moving. After 10 minutes of stirring, add mazetta or marshmallow creme. If you intend to flavor the entire batch one flavor, you can add the flavoring and/or nuts anytime after adding the mazetta. Stir until fondant becomes very stiff and loses its gloss. At this point it has set up.

If it is too stiff to handle, break off small pieces and work in your hands like modeling clay. This should cause it to soften. You could also wrap the fondant in plastic wrap and cover it with a warm damp tea towel for 15 minutes. If it doesn't soften it may be overcooked. Follow directions for recooking fondant on page 17.

If you have stirred the fondant for more than 1 hour and it hasn't set up, try letting it rest for a few minutes without stirring. This will sometimes cause the fondant to begin the desired crystallization process. If resting the fondant doesn't work, it may be undercooked. Follow directions for recooking on page 17.

Honey Buttercream Fondant Flavor Variations
The following variations are based on flavoring an entire batch one flavor. If you are dividing it into several different flavors, reduce the amounts of flavorings accordingly. The amount of coloring used is a matter of personal preference.

For Vanilla or Vanilla Nut—Add 1 tablespoon vanilla and 1 cup chopped pecans or walnuts.

For Black Walnut—Add 1 tablespoon vanilla, 1/4 teaspoon black walnut extract and 1 cup chopped walnuts.

For Cherry Creams—Add 2 teaspoons almond extract and 1 teaspoon rum extract.

For Cherry Nut—Add 2 teaspoons almond extract, 1 teaspoon rum extract, 1/2 cup chopped candied cherries and 1 cup chopped pecans, walnuts or almonds.

For Mint Creams—Add 1/2 teaspoon oil of peppermint or 2 teaspoons peppermint extract.

For Lemon Creams—Add 1 tablespoon lemon extract, a small amount of yellow food color and 1/2 teaspoon citric acid.

For Orange Creams—Add 1 tablespoon orange extract, 2 to 3 drops of orange food color and 1/2 teaspoon citric acid.

For Raspberry Creams—Add 2 tablespoons raspberry extract, 1/4 teaspoon lemon extract, 8 drops pink food color or 1 drop red food color, and 1/2 teaspoon citric acid.

Making several flavors from one batch

After Honey Buttercream Fondant has set up, divide it into 2 or 3 balls. Press your thumb into the center of one of the portions of fondant, creating a small hole. Pour desired flavoring and food color into hole and knead with your hands until thoroughly mixed. You may also work in nuts at this time.

Sometimes the fondant becomes too sticky to handle. If it does, wash your hands and dry them thoroughly. Dust your hands with cornstarch or flour; powdered sugar makes them stickier.

Shaping fondants into centers

When fondant is flavored and set up, it is ready for forming into centers for chocolates, or for storage. Cover 2 trays or baking sheets with waxed paper; set aside. To shape fondant for centers, break off approximately 1/2 cup of fondant. Roll the fondant into a rope 1/2 inch thick. With a table knife, cut into 1-inch pieces.

Place the pieces one at a time in the palms of your hands and roll into balls. Arrange the balls on the waxed paper-lined trays. Continue until all fondant is rolled out. With your finger tips, slightly flatten each ball. This will give a more professional look to the finished chocolates.

The fondant centers are ready to dip immediately, or could stand overnight at room temperature, if desired. If your fondant is very soft, let the centers stand for several hours to form a crust before dipping. To dip, see information in the Chocolate chapter (beginning on page 146).

If you are going to store fondant, wrap it in plastic wrap or place it in a plastic bag. Fondant can be stored in the refrigerator for several weeks or frozen for several months. Allow it to warm to room temperature before unwrapping. Proceed as directed above for shaping the centers. Makes about 100 centers.

Browned Butter Fondant

Makes a smooth, creamy and buttery chocolate center. Finish either by coating with tempered dipping chocolate (page 150) or use this fondant for pecan log centers (page 70).

1/4 cup butter
1 cup whipping cream
3 tablespoons light corn syrup
4 cups sugar

1/2 cup milk
2 tablespoons butter
1 teaspoon vanilla

Set aside a 9" x 13" ungreased baking pan. In a heavy 4-quart saucepan, cook 1/4 cup butter over medium-high heat until golden-brown. Remove from heat and allow to cool for 2 minutes. Add cream, corn syrup and sugar. Place over medium heat and stir gently but constantly with a wooden spoon until mixture comes to a boil. If sugar crystals have formed, wash down sides of pan with a wet pastry brush. Rinse spoon well to make sure no sugar granules remain.

Clip on candy thermometer. Cook, stirring constantly with wooden spoon, to 258F (125C) or hard-ball stage. Still stirring, slowly add milk, which will reduce the temperature. Cook to 238F (115C) or soft-ball stage. Remove from heat and, without stirring or scraping, pour into baking pan. Without excess movement, place in refrigerator or other cool area.

When bottom of pan no longer feels warm, begin stirring fondant with a wooden spoon. Add 2 tablespoons butter and the vanilla. Stir the fondant until it loses its shine and begins to set up. It resembles thick frosting at this point. It sometimes sets up in as little as 15 minutes, but generally takes 30 to 40 minutes of stirring.

If, after stirring, it hardens too much, wrap the fondant in plastic wrap and cover it with a warm damp tea towel for 15 minutes. This should cause it to soften. Sometimes you may find that lumps form in the fondant and you have to knead it like bread dough. If the fondant won't soften, you probably overcooked it. Follow the directions on page 17 for recooking.

If you have stirred the fondant for more than 1 hour and it hasn't set up, try letting it rest for a few minutes without stirring. This will sometimes cause the fondant to begin the desired crystallization process. If resting the fondant doesn't work, it may be undercooked. Follow directions for recooking on page 17.

Scrape onto plastic wrap and store in the refrigerator; or shape to form chocolate centers (see page 23) or use for pecan log centers. Makes about 100 centers for chocolates or 25 pecan logs.

Apricot Cream Fondant

A tasty fondant with a pale orange color, this is one of Pauline's specialties.

1 cup whipping cream
1/2 cup milk
1/3 cup light corn syrup
4 cups sugar
1/4 teaspoon salt
3/4 cup Mazetta (page 82) or
   marshmallow creme
1/2 cup firmly packed, finely chopped
   dried apricots

1 teaspoon almond extract
1/2 teaspoon orange extract
1 drop orange food color
1/2 teaspoon dry or liquid citric acid
1 cup chopped roasted almonds,
   if desired
Cornstarch or all-purpose flour (optional)

Set aside a 9" x 13" ungreased baking pan. In a heavy 4-quart saucepan, combine cream, milk, corn syrup, sugar and salt. Place over high heat and stir with a wooden spoon until mixture comes to a boil. If sugar crystals are present, wash down sides of pan with a wet pastry brush.

Clip on candy thermometer. Stirring occasionally, cook over high heat to 238F (115C) or soft-ball stage. Remove from heat and, without stirring or scraping, pour into baking pan. Without excess movement, place in refrigerator or other cool location.

When bottom of pan no longer feels warm, begin stirring fondant with a wooden spoon. You don't have to stir rapidly, just keep the mass moving. After 15 minutes of stirring, mix in mazetta or marshmallow creme. Stir in apricots, extracts, food color, citric acid and almonds anytime after the mazetta is mixed in. Stir until fondant becomes very stiff and loses its gloss. At this point it has set up.

If it is too stiff to handle, break off small pieces and work in your hands like modeling clay. This should cause it to soften. You could also wrap in plastic wrap and cover with a warm damp tea towel for 15 minutes. If it doesn't soften it may be overcooked. Follow directions for recooking fondant on page 17. If you have stirred the fondant for more than 1 hour and it hasn't set up, try letting it rest for a few minutes without stirring. This will sometimes cause the fondant to begin the desired crystallization process. If resting the fondant doesn't work, it may be undercooked. Follow directions for recooking on page 17.

When fondant is flavored and set up, it is ready for forming into centers for chocolates, or for storage. Cover 2 trays or baking sheets with waxed paper; set aside. To shape fondant for centers, break off approximately 1/2 cup of fondant. Roll the fondant into a rope 1/2 inch thick. With a table knife, cut into 1-inch pieces.

Place the pieces one at a time in the palms of your hands and roll into balls. (This fondant sometimes becomes sticky. If it does, wash your hands and dry them thoroughly. Dust hands with cornstarch or flour—powdered sugar makes them stickier—before shaping.) Arrange the balls on the waxed paper-lined trays. Continue until all fondant is rolled out. With your finger tips, slightly flatten each ball. This will give a more professional look to the finished chocolates.

The fondant centers are ready to dip immediately, or could stand at room temperature overnight, if desired. If your fondant is very soft, let the centers stand for several hours to form a crust before dipping. To dip, see information in the Chocolate chapter (beginning on page 146).

If you are going to store fondant, wrap it in plastic wrap or place it in a plastic bag. Fondant can be stored in the refrigerator for several weeks or frozen for several months. Allow it to warm to room temperature before unwrapping. Proceed as directed above for shaping the centers. Makes about 100 centers.

Grand Opera Creams

In addition to dipped chocolates, the slight caramel flavor in this fondant makes it excellent for Pecan Logs (page 70).

1 cup whipping cream
1-1/2 cups milk, divided
1/2 cup light corn syrup
4 cups sugar

1/4 teaspoon salt
1/2 cup Mazetta (page 82) or
   marshmallow creme, if desired
1 tablespoon vanilla

Set aside a 9" x 13" ungreased baking pan. In a heavy 4-quart saucepan, combine cream, 1 cup of the milk, corn syrup, sugar and salt. Place over low heat and stir with a wooden spoon until mixture comes to a boil. If sugar crystals are present, wash down sides of pan with a wet pastry brush.

Clip on candy thermometer. Stirring occasionally, cook over low heat until mixture turns a medium-tan color, about 30 minutes. Stirring constantly, slowly pour in the remaining 1/2 cup milk and continue cooking to 238F (115C) or soft-ball stage. Remove from heat and, without stirring or scraping, pour into baking pan. Without excess movement, place in refrigerator or other cool area.

When bottom of pan is just slightly warm, begin stirring fondant with a wooden spoon. You don't have to stir rapidly, just keep the mass moving. If desired, after 15 minutes of stirring mix in mazetta or marshmallow creme. If you intend to flavor the entire batch one flavor, you can add the extract and/or nuts anytime after adding the mazetta. Stir until fondant becomes very stiff and loses its gloss. At this point it has set up.

If it is too stiff to handle, break off small pieces and work in your hands like modeling clay. This should cause it to soften. You could also wrap in plastic wrap and cover with a warm damp tea towel for 15 minutes. If it doesn't soften it may be overcooked. Follow directions for recooking fondant on page 17.

If you have stirred the fondant for more than 1 hour and it hasn't set up, try letting it rest for a few minutes without stirring. This will sometimes cause the fondant to begin the desired crystallization process. If resting the fondant doesn't work, it may be undercooked. Follow directions for recooking on page 17.

Grand Opera Creams Variations
These amounts are for the entire batch to be flavored one flavor. If you are going to divide the batch, reduce the flavoring amounts accordingly.
For Maple or Maple-Nut—Add 1 tablespoon maple and 1 cup chopped pecans or walnuts.
For Rum or Rum-Nut—Add 1 tablespoon rum extract and 1 cup chopped pecans or walnuts.
For Date-Nut—Add 1 tablespoon vanilla, 1 cup chopped dates and 1/2 cup chopped nuts.

Making several flavors from one batch
After Grand Opera Creams fondant has set up, divide it into 2 or 3 balls. Press your thumb into the center of one of the portions, creating a small hole. Pour in desired flavoring and knead with your hands until it is well-mixed. You may also work in nuts at this time.

Sometimes the fondant becomes too sticky to handle. If it does, wash your hands and dry them thoroughly. Dust your hands with cornstarch or flour; powdered sugar makes them stickier.

When fondant is flavored and set up, it is ready for forming into centers for chocolates, or for storage. Cover 2 trays or baking sheets with waxed paper; set aside. To shape for centers, break off approximately 1/2 cup of fondant. Roll the fondant into a rope 1/2 inch thick. With a table knife, cut into 1-inch pieces.

Place the pieces one at a time in the palms of your hands and roll into balls. Arrange the balls on the waxed paper-lined trays. Continue until all fondant is rolled out. With your finger tips, slightly flatten each ball. This will give a more professional look to the finished chocolates.

The fondant centers are ready to dip immediately, or could stand at room temperature overnight, if desired. If your fondant is very soft, let the centers stand for several hours to form a crust before dipping. To dip, see information in the Chocolate chapter starting on page 146; for Pecan Logs, see page 70.

If you are going to store fondant, wrap it in plastic wrap or place it in a plastic bag. Fondant can be stored in the refrigerator for several weeks or frozen for several months. Allow it to warm to room temperature before unwrapping. Proceed as directed above for shaping the centers. Makes 100 chocolate centers or 25 pecan log centers.

Boston Creams

Caramelized sugar gives this candy a delicate flavor.

2 cups sugar, divided   **3 tablespoons butter**
1 (12-ounce) can evaporated milk, divided

Pour 1 cup of the sugar into a heavy 9-inch skillet. Place over high heat and caramelize the sugar by stirring with a wooden spoon until it turns into a golden syrup. *Be very careful as this syrup is extremely hot and could burn the skin.* Reduce heat to low and, stirring constantly, add 2/3 cup evaporated milk.

Stir in remaining cup of sugar, bring to boil and boil 1 minute. Stir in remaining milk. Cook, stirring constantly, to 244F (115C) or firm-ball stage. (If using thermometer, hold upright and immerse bulb in syrup for accurate reading.) Remove from heat and allow mixture to stand undisturbed for 5 minutes. Add butter and begin stirring with a wooden spoon. Stir until it creams and sets up. Scrape onto plastic wrap. Pat into a log shape about 1 inch in diameter. Seal and place in refrigerator, or slice and serve immediately. Makes 50 slices (or about 50 centers for chocolates).

Variations
Add 1/2 cup chopped nuts when candy creams.
Add 1/2 cup toasted coconut when candy creams.
Roll logs in chopped nuts.
Dip in tempered dipping chocolate (pages 146-153) or in melted compound coating (pages 134, 146-153).

On the following pages: a "centerfold" of assorted chocolate-dipped fondants. From left: Double-Dipped Mint Creams (pages 24, 26, 28 and 153); Vanilla Nut (pages 24 and 28); Coconut Creams (page 26); and Chocolate Fondant (page 36).

Chocolate Fondant

Doubly delicious dipped in chocolate.

1 cup whipping cream
1/2 cup milk
1/4 cup light corn syrup
3 (1-ounce) squares unsweetened
   baking chocolate *or*
   1/3 cup unsweetened cocoa

4 cups sugar
1/4 teaspoon salt
1/2 cup Mazetta (page 82) or
   marshmallow creme, if desired
Flavoring and nuts (variations follow)

Set aside a 9" x 13" ungreased baking pan. In a heavy 4-quart saucepan, combine cream, milk, corn syrup, chocolate or cocoa, sugar and salt. Place over high heat and stir occasionally with a wooden spoon until mixture comes to a boil. If sugar crystals are present, wash down sides of pan with a wet pastry brush.

Clip on candy thermometer. Cook syrup to 236F (115C) or soft-ball stage. Remove from heat and, without stirring or scraping, pour into baking pan. Without excess movement, place in refrigerator or in other cool area.

When bottom of pan no longer feels warm, begin stirring fondant with a wooden spoon. You don't have to stir rapidly, just keep the mass moving. If desired, after 15 minutes of stirring add mazetta or marshmallow creme. If you intend to flavor the entire batch one flavor, you can add the flavoring and/or nuts anytime after the mazetta is added. Stir until fondant becomes very stiff and loses its gloss. At this point it has set up.

If it is too stiff to handle, break off small pieces and work them in your hands like modeling clay. This should cause it to soften. You could also wrap the fondant in plastic wrap and cover it with a warm damp tea towel for 15 minutes. This will also cause it to soften. If it doesn't, it may be overcooked. Follow directions for recooking fondant on page 17.

If you have stirred the fondant for more than 1 hour and it hasn't set up, try letting it rest for a few minutes without stirring. This will sometimes cause the fondant to begin the desired crystallization process. If resting the fondant doesn't work, it may be undercooked. Follow directions for recooking on page 17.

Chocolate Fondant Flavor Variations
The following variations are based on flavoring an entire batch one flavor. If you are dividing it into several different flavors, reduce the amounts of flavorings accordingly.
For Chocolate Nut—Add 1 tablespoon vanilla and 1 cup chopped pecans or walnuts.
For Almond Fudge—Add 2 teaspoons maple extract and 1 cup chopped roasted almonds.
For Chocolate Marshmallow—Add 1 tablespoon vanilla and 1 cup miniature marshmallows.
For Chocolate Mint—Add 1/2 teaspoon oil of peppermint.

Making several flavors from one batch
After Chocolate Fondant has set up, divide it into 2 or 3 balls. Press your thumb into the center of one of the portions, creating a small hole. Pour in desired flavoring and knead with your hands until it is well-mixed. You may also work in nuts at this time.

Sometimes the fondant becomes too sticky to handle. If this happens, wash hands and dry them thoroughly. Dust hands with cornstarch or flour; powdered sugar makes fondant stickier.

Shaping fondant into centers

When fondant is flavored and set up, it is ready for forming into centers for chocolates, or for storage. Cover 2 trays or baking sheets with waxed paper; set aside. To shape fondant for centers, break off approximately 1/2 cup of fondant. Roll the fondant into a rope 1/2 inch thick. With a table knife, cut the candy into 1-inch pieces.

Place the pieces one at a time in the palms of your hands and roll them into balls. Place the balls of fondant onto the waxed paper-lined trays. Continue until all the fondant is rolled out. With your finger tips, slightly flatten each ball. This will give a more professional look to the finished chocolates.

The fondant centers are ready to dip immediately or they can stand overnight, if desired. If your fondant is very soft, let the centers stand for several hours to form a crust before dipping. To dip, see information in the Chocolate chapter (beginning on page 146).

If you are going to store fondant, wrap it in plastic wrap or place it in a plastic bag. Fondant can be stored in the refrigerator for several weeks or frozen for several months. Allow it to warm to room temperature before unwrapping. Proceed as directed above for shaping the centers. Makes about 100 chocolate centers.

Pineapple Fondant

Drain the pineapple well to keep this fondant from becoming too sticky.

1 (20-ounce) can crushed pineapple	**2 tablespoons butter**
1 cup whipping cream	**4 cups sugar**
1/4 cup light corn syrup	**Cornstarch or all-purpose flour (optional)**

Set aside a 9" x 13" ungreased baking pan. Thoroughly drain pineapple, reserving 1 cup juice; add water, if necessary, to measure a total of 1 cup liquid. Spread pineapple between several layers of paper towels. Press firmly to remove as much liquid as possible. When pressed dry, the pineapple will appear very flat; set aside.

In a heavy 4-quart saucepan, combine pineapple juice, cream, corn syrup, butter and sugar. Place over medium-high heat and stir occasionally with a wooden spoon until mixture comes to a boil. If sugar crystals are present, wash down sides of pan with a wet pastry brush.

Clip on candy thermometer. Cook over medium-high heat to 242F (120C) or firm-ball stage. Remove from heat and, without stirring or scraping, pour into baking pan. Without excess movement, place in refrigerator or other cool area.

When bottom of pan no longer feels warm, begin stirring fondant with a wooden spoon. (If using the same spoon used for stirring syrup, make sure it is thoroughly rinsed to remove all sugar granules.) You don't have to stir rapidly, just keep the mass moving. Add the dry pineapple. Stir until fondant becomes very stiff and loses its gloss. At this point it has set up.

This fondant sometimes becomes very sticky. If it does, wash your hands and dry them thoroughly. Dust hands with cornstarch or flour—powdered sugar makes them stickier— before shaping.

Shaping fondant into centers

When Pineapple Fondant is set up, it is ready for forming into centers for chocolates. Cover 2 trays or baking sheets with waxed paper; set aside. To shape fondant for centers, break off approximately 1/2 cup of fondant. Roll the fondant into a rope 1/2 inch thick. With a table knife, cut the candy into 1-inch pieces.

Place the pieces one at a time in the palms of your hands and roll into balls. Arrange the balls on the waxed paper-lined trays. Continue until all fondant is rolled out. With your finger tips, slightly flatten each ball. This will give a more professional look to the finished chocolates.

These fondant centers should be dipped within a few hours as the fruit will cause the fondant to become overly soft if it is not protected by a coating. To dip, see information in the Chocolate chapter (beginning on page 146). Makes 100 chocolate centers.

Variations

For an unusual center, combine equal amounts of Pineapple Fondant and Daphne's Divinity (page 77). Knead them together and form as you would for any other center.

For Pineapple-Coconut—Add 1 cup flaked coconut along with the pineapple.

Lemon Honey Fondant

A delightful combination of honey and lemon. This fondant is especially good dipped in dark chocolate.

2/3 cup water
2 tablespoons light, mild honey
2 cups sugar
3 tablespoons butter
1/8 teaspoon cream of tartar

1/2 cup Mazetta (page 82) or
   marshmallow creme, divided
1 teaspoon lemon extract
1/4 teaspoon citric acid

In a heavy 2-quart saucepan, combine water, honey, sugar, butter and cream of tartar. Place over high heat and stir with a wooden spoon until mixture comes to a boil. If sugar crystals are present, wash down sides of pan with a wet pastry brush.

Clip on candy thermometer. Cook syrup to 240F(115C) or soft-ball stage. Remove pan from heat; remove wooden spoon and thermometer. Cool pan quickly by placing in several inches of cold water. Don't move candy needlessly; even slight movement can start crystallization too early and your candy will have coarse grains of sugar.

When mixture is cool, add 1/4 cup of the mazetta or marshmallow creme and begin stirring with a wooden spoon. Stir until it holds its shape, about 10 minutes. Add lemon extract, citric acid and remaining 1/4 cup mazetta. Stir until fondant becomes too thick to mix and it sets up.

Variations
For Peppermint—Add 6 drops oil of peppermint in place of lemon extract, and omit the citric acid.
For Orange—Substitute 1 teaspoon orange extract for the lemon extract.

Shaping fondant into centers
When fondant is flavored and set up, it is ready for forming into centers for chocolates, or for storage. Cover tray or baking sheet with waxed paper; set aside. To shape for centers, break off approximately 1/2 cup of fondant. Roll the fondant into a rope 1/2 inch thick. With a table knife, cut the candy into 1-inch pieces.

Place the pieces one at a time in the palms of your hands and roll into balls. Arrange the balls on the waxed paper-lined tray. Continue until all the fondant is rolled out. With your finger tips, slightly flatten each ball. This will give a more professional look to the finished chocolates.

The fondant centers are ready to dip immediately or they can stand at room temperature overnight, if desired. If your fondant is very soft, let the centers stand for several hours to form a crust before dipping. To dip, see information in the Chocolate chapter (beginning on page 146).

If you are going to store fondant, wrap it in plastic wrap or place it in a plastic bag. Fondant can be stored in the refrigerator for several weeks or frozen for several months. Allow it to warm to room temperature before unwrapping.

This fondant sometimes develops a slight grain, but it will mellow out after dipping. This candy actually improves with age; after dipping, it can be stored in a cool room—60F (15C)—for at least 6 weeks. Makes 50 chocolate centers.

Brown Sugar Fondant

A delightful penouche candy! If you like a stronger flavor, increase the amount of brown sugar and decrease the granulated sugar by the same amount.

1 cup whipping cream
1/2 cup milk
1/4 cup light corn syrup
3 cups granulated sugar
1 cup firmly packed brown sugar

1/4 teaspoon salt
1/2 cup Mazetta (page 82) or
 marshmallow creme, if desired
Extract(s) and/or chopped nuts
 (variations follow)

Set aside a 9" x 13" ungreased baking pan. In a heavy 4-quart saucepan, combine cream, milk, corn syrup, sugars and salt. Place over medium-high heat and stir with a wooden spoon until mixture comes to a boil. If any sugar crystals are present, wash down sides of pan with a wet pastry brush.

Clip on candy thermometer. Stirring occasionally, cook to 236F (115C) or soft-ball stage. Remove from heat and, without stirring or scraping, pour into baking pan. Without excess movement, place in refrigerator or other cool location.

When bottom of pan no longer feels warm, begin stirring fondant with a wooden spoon. You don't have to stir rapidly, just keep the mass moving. If desired, after 15 minutes of stirring mix in mazetta or marshmallow creme. If you intend to make the entire batch one flavor, you can add the extract and nuts anytime after the mazetta has been mixed in. Stir until fondant becomes very stiff and loses its gloss. At this point it has set up.

If it is too stiff to handle, break off small pieces and work in your hands like modeling clay. This should cause it to soften. You could also wrap in plastic wrap and cover with a warm damp tea towel for 15 minutes. If it doesn't soften it may be overcooked. Follow directions for recooking fondant on page 17.

If you have stirred the fondant for more than 1 hour and it hasn't set up, try letting it rest for a few minutes without stirring. This will sometimes cause the fondant to begin the desired crystallization process. If resting the fondant doesn't work, it may be undercooked. Follow directions for recooking on page 17.

Brown Sugar Fondant Flavor Variations
The following variations are based on flavoring an entire batch one flavor. If you are dividing it into several different flavors, reduce the amounts of flavorings accordingly.
For Maple Nut—Add 1 tablespoon maple extract and 1 cup chopped pecans or walnuts.
For Penouche—Add 1 tablespoon vanilla, and 1 cup chopped pecans if desired.
For Rum—Add 2 teaspoons rum extract (real rum will cause the candy to ferment).
For Date-Nut—Add 1 tablespoon vanilla, 1 cup chopped dates and 1/2 cup chopped nuts.

Making several flavors from one batch
After Brown Sugar Fondant has set up, divide it into 2 or 3 balls. Press your thumb into the center of one of the portions, creating a small hole. Pour in desired flavoring and knead with your hands until it is well-mixed. You may also work in nuts at this time.

Sometimes the fondant becomes too sticky to handle. If it does, wash your hands and dry them thoroughly. Dust your hands with cornstarch or flour; powdered sugar makes fondant stickier.

Shaping fondant into centers

When fondant is flavored and set up, it is ready for forming into centers for chocolates, or for storage. Cover 2 trays or baking sheets with waxed paper; set aside. To shape for centers, break off approximately 1/2 cup of fondant. Roll the fondant into a rope 1/2 inch thick. With a table knife, cut the candy into 1-inch pieces.

Place the pieces one at a time in the palms of your hands and roll into balls. Place the balls on the waxed paper-lined trays. Continue until all the fondant is rolled out. With your finger tips, slightly flatten each ball. This will give a more professional look to the finished chocolates.

The fondant centers are ready to dip immediately or they can stand at room temperature overnight, if desired. If your fondant is very soft, let the centers stand for several hours to form a crust before dipping. To dip, see information in the Chocolate chapter (beginning on page 146).

If you are going to store fondant, wrap it in plastic wrap or place it in a plastic bag. Fondant can be stored in the refrigerator for several weeks or frozen for several months. Allow it to warm to room temperature before unwrapping. Proceed as described above for shaping the centers. Makes about 100 chocolate centers.

No-Cook Fondant

Too busy to try the cooked fondants? Try this easy version.

2/3 cup soft butter
2/3 cup light corn syrup
1/2 teaspoon salt
About 1 teaspoon extract

2 pounds powdered sugar
About 100 pecan halves or candied cherries,
 or a combination

Line 2 large baking sheets or trays with waxed paper; set aside. In a large bowl, combine butter, corn syrup, salt and extract. Stir with a wooden spoon, gradually working in powdered sugar. When mixture is too stiff for a spoon, begin kneading as for bread dough. When all the powdered sugar has been added, continue kneading until fondant is smooth. Form into balls 3/4 inch in diameter and place on waxed paper-lined trays.

If desired, dip in tempered dipping chocolate (pages 146-153) or roll in nuts. Press pecan half or candied cherry on each piece. Unless this fondant is dipped in chocolate, it will dry out if not eaten within a few hours. Makes about 100 pieces.

Melted Cordial Fondant

This is the "liquid" in cherry cordials. Note that there is no fat in this recipe and sugar crystals will form easily if the pan is not properly washed down. This fondant does tend to set up much firmer than the basic cream fondant on page 24.

1-1/2 cups water	4 cups sugar
1/3 cup light corn syrup	Pinch of salt

Set aside a 9" x 13" ungreased baking pan. In a 4-quart saucepan, combine water, corn syrup, sugar and salt. Place over high heat and stir with a wooden spoon until mixture comes to a boil. Wash down sides of pan with a wet pastry brush. *Remember, there is no fat in this recipe and sugar crystals will form easily if not completely dissolved.*

Clip on candy thermometer. Cook without stirring to 240F (115C) or soft-ball stage. Remove from heat and, without stirring or scraping, pour into baking pan. Without excess movement, place in refrigerator or other cool area.

When bottom of pan no longer feels warm, begin stirring fondant with a wooden spoon. Stir until fondant sets up, usually about 15 to 20 minutes.

If fondant sets up too hard, wrap it in plastic wrap, cover with a warm damp tea towel and let it rest 15 to 45 minutes. This will cause it to soften. When soft, use fondant immediately or place in a plastic bag and store in a cool place for up to several weeks. To make cherry cordials, follow directions on pages 86-88. Makes enough centers for about 125 chocolates.

Fresh Raspberry Fondant

This candy has a delicious, fresh, slightly tart flavor that gets even better and creamier 2 or 3 weeks after it's made. The texture is not quite as fluffy as the other cream fondants—it sometimes has a slight grain at first, but this will disappear—and it keeps at least 2 months.

1 cup whipping cream	1/4 teaspoon citric acid
3 tablespoons light corn syrup	1/3 cup Mazetta (page 82) or marshmallow creme
3 cups sugar	
1/8 teaspoon salt	2 to 3 tablespoons thick raspberry jam
Pinch of baking soda	Powdered sugar, if needed
1 cup (packed but not squeezed) fresh or frozen thawed raspberries, drained, if necessary	

Set aside a 9" X 13" ungreased baking pan. In a heavy 3-quart saucepan, combine cream, corn syrup, sugar, salt, baking soda and raspberries. Place over high heat and stir constantly with a wooden spoon until mixture comes to a boil. If sugar crystals are present, wash down sides of pan with a wet pastry brush.

Clip on candy thermometer. Cook syrup to 240F (115C) or soft-ball stage. Remove from heat and, without stirring or scraping, pour into baking pan. Without excess movement, place in refrigerator or other cool area.

When bottom of pan feels *lukewarm*, begin stirring fondant with a wooden spoon. You don't have to stir rapidly, just enough to keep the mass moving. Stir in citric acid and gradually add mazetta as you beat. Stir until fondant begins to set—this usually takes about 20 minutes—and then add jam, mixing it thoroughly into the fondant. Continue stirring until fondant becomes very stiff and loses its gloss. At this point it has set up.

If the fondant refuses to set up, possibly due to undercooking, add powdered sugar 2 to 3 tablespoons at a time and stir well; wait 5 minutes to see if additional powdered sugar is needed.

Shaping fondant into centers

When fondant is set up, it is ready for forming into centers for chocolates, or for storage. Cover 2 trays or baking sheets with waxed paper; set aside. To shape fondant for centers, break off approximately 1/2 cup of fondant. Roll the fondant into a rope 1/2 inch thick. With a table knife, cut the candy into 1-inch pieces.

Place the pieces one at a time in the palms of your hands and roll them into balls. Place the balls of fondant onto the waxed paper-lined trays. Continue until all the fondant is rolled out. With your finger tips, slightly flatten each ball. This will give a more professional look to the finished chocolates.

The fondant centers are ready to dip immediately or they can stand overnight, if desired; they may also be served plain without being dipped. If your fondant is very soft, let the centers stand for several hours to form a crust before dipping. To dip, see information in the Chocolate chapter (beginning on page 146).

If you are going to store fondant, wrap it in plastic wrap or place it in a plastic bag. Fondant can be stored in the refrigerator for several weeks or frozen for several months. Allow it to warm to room temperature before unwrapping. Proceed as directed above for shaping the centers. Makes 60 to 70 centers.

Variations
For Strawberry—Use 1 cup sliced strawberries in place of the raspberries, and stir in 1/2 teaspoon strawberry extract and 2 to 3 tablespoons thick strawberry jam.
For Raspberry Nut or Strawberry Nut—Stir in about 3/4 cup chopped pecans or walnuts along with the jam.

A tempting truffle, dipped in milk chocolate and drizzled with pink compound coating (page 47).

Truffles & Fudges

Probably the most elegant candies that you can make are truffles. They require little cooking, very little candymaking experience, and people invariably "ooh" and "aah" over them.

Silky smooth, light and creamy, this confection is usually dipped in chocolate, or rolled in chopped nuts, cocoa powder, coconut or chocolate shot. Truffles will not stay fresh as long as other types of candy, but we guarantee they will be eaten long before they have a chance to dry out. This type of candy must be kept cool and, unless frozen, should be eaten within two weeks.

Everyone remembers making fudge as a child. Without a doubt, more fudge is made in homes than any other candy. With our recipes we guarantee you will have success every time. Our newer recipes call for marshmallow creme or compound coating so the problem of coarse graining is completely eliminated.

Old-fashioned fudge is similar to fondant and must be handled accordingly: cooled rapidly without stirring, then beaten until creamy. Fudges are stirred while there is still warmth in the batch. This causes the slight grain that is traditional in this type of candy. We have included time-tested recipes for beaten fudges, as well as our quicker, easier, foolproof recipes. Whether your palate prefers plain chocolate, peanut butter or a variation, you will find new favorite recipes here.

Brown & White Truffle Squares

An excellent—and economical—candy for summer as it holds its shape in the heat.

1 pound (about 2-1/2 cups) white compound
   coating, melted
1 pound (about 2-1/2 cups)
   chocolate-flavored compound coating,
   melted

3/4 cup evaporated milk
1/4 cup margarine
1 teaspoon vanilla

Line an 8-inch square baking pan with plastic wrap; set aside. Place melted coatings in separate medium-size bowls. Combine milk and margarine in a 1-quart saucepan. Place over medium heat until margarine is melted. Remove from heat. Pour 1/2 cup of the milk mixture over white coating. Add vanilla and mix with electric mixer until well-blended. Pour into prepared pan and spread evenly. Refrigerate to set.

Add remaining 1/2 cup milk mixture to chocolate coating and beat until mixture is well-blended. Spoon carefully over the first layer, spreading until smooth. Refrigerate 24 hours or until firm. Cut into 1-inch squares and serve immediately. Store in refrigerator. Makes 64 pieces.

Note: To form truffles into "marbleized" balls, see note on page 47.

Variations
Use 6 drops oil of peppermint in place of the vanilla.
Use 1 teaspoon of your favorite extract in place of the vanilla.
Use different-colored and flavored coatings in place of either the white or the chocolate layer.

Berry Truffles

If you like berries and cream, you'll love these truffles.

1/3 cup whipping cream
3/4 pound white chocolate (not compound
   coating), melted

1/4 teaspoon citric acid
1/3 cup strawberry or raspberry jam

Line an 8-inch square baking pan with plastic wrap; set aside. Heat cream in a 1-quart saucepan over low heat until it begins to steam; do not allow it to boil. Remove from heat and let stand until slightly cooled but still very warm. Place melted white chocolate in a medium-size bowl. Pour warm cream over chocolate and beat with electric mixer until well-blended. Add citric acid and jam. Continue mixing until jam is incorporated. Spoon into prepared pan. Refrigerate 2 hours or until firm. Cut into 1-inch squares and serve immediately. Store in refrigerator. Makes 64 pieces.

Note: To form truffles into balls, see note on page 47.

Elegant Chocolate Truffles

Wonderfully delicious and wonderfully easy.

**1-1/2 pounds (about 4-1/2 cups) milk chocolate,
melted (110F/45C)**
1 cup whipping cream
1-1/2 teaspoons vanilla

Line an 8-inch square baking pan with plastic wrap; set aside. Place melted chocolate in a medium-size bowl. In a 1-quart saucepan, scald cream. Remove from heat and let cool for 5 minutes. Stir in vanilla. Beat chocolate with an electric mixer. Stop mixer and pour cream all at once over chocolate. Continue beating, cleaning sides and bottom of bowl several times with rubber scraper, until mixture is smooth and well-blended; this takes no more than 1 to 2 minutes. Pour into prepared pan and refrigerate 6 hours or until firm. Cut into 1-inch squares and serve immediately. Store in refrigerator. Makes 64 pieces.

Variations
For Mint Truffles—Add 5 drops oil of peppermint in place of vanilla.
For Cherry Nut Truffles—Add 1 teaspoon almond extract in place of vanilla, and stir in 3/4 cup chopped candied cherries and 1 cup chopped walnuts, pecans or almonds.

Note: To form truffles into balls, omit 8-inch pan and chill mixture in bowl until firm. Shape into balls with spoon and hands or with small ice cream scoop; if mixture becomes too soft to form, wash and thoroughly dry hands and dust lightly with cornstarch. Arrange truffles on waxed paper-lined baking sheet. Dip in tempered dipping chocolate (pages 146-153) or melted compound coating (pages 134, 146-153), or roll in unsweetened cocoa, chopped nuts or coconut. To decorate, use melted compound coating. Spoon into a pastry bag fitted with a small tip or into a plastic bag; cut a small hole in the end of the plastic bag. Pipe coating in "drizzles" over the set chocolate. Makes 24 to 36 truffles, depending upon size desired.

The chocolate-and-cream mixture may sometimes develop a rough, somewhat "curdled" look as the truffles are beaten.

To correct this situation, simply beat in more milk or cream—it does not need to be heated and may take anywhere from 2 tablespoons to about 1/2 cup—and continue beating until the mixture is smooth.

Snow Queen Truffles

These white chocolate truffles literally melt in your mouth.

2/3 cup whipping cream
1-1/2 pounds (about 4-1/2 cups) white chocolate, melted (110F/45C)
1/2 teaspoon vanilla, mint, orange or rum extract

Tempered dipping chocolate (pages 146-153) or melted compound coating (pages 134, 146-153)

Line an 8-inch square baking pan with plastic wrap; set aside. Heat cream in a 1-quart saucepan over low heat until it begins to steam; do not allow it to boil. Remove from heat and let stand until slightly cooled but still very warm. Place melted white chocolate in a medium-size bowl. Pour warm cream over chocolate and beat with electric mixer until well-blended. Add extract and mix well. Spoon into prepared pan. Refrigerate 2 hours or until firm. Cut into 1-inch squares. Dip in tempered chocolate or melted compound coating. Store in refrigerator. Makes 64 pieces.

Note: To form truffles into balls, see note on page 47.

Melissa's Peanut Butter Truffles

My daughter Melissa's favorite candy.

1 cup whipping cream
1-1/2 pounds (about 4-1/2 cups) milk chocolate, melted

1/3 cup creamy peanut butter
Tempered dipping chocolate (pages 146-153), if desired

Line an 8-inch square baking pan with plastic wrap; set aside. In a 1-quart saucepan, scald cream. Remove from heat and add peanut butter. Transfer melted chocolate to a medium-size bowl. Pour cream mixture over the top. Using electric mixer, beat until thick and well-blended. Pour into prepared pan. Refrigerate 2 hours or until firm. Cut into 1-inch squares. Serve plain, or dip in tempered chocolate. Store in refrigerator. Makes 64 pieces.

Note: To form truffles into balls, see note on page 47.

Variation
Use crunchy peanut butter in place of creamy.

Fruit-Flavored Truffles

Use any fruit-flavored gelatin to vary the flavor.

1 cup whipping cream
1 (3-ounce) package fruit-flavored gelatin
1 pound (about 2-1/2 cups) white compound
   coating, melted

1/4 teaspoon fruit-flavored extract (use same
   flavor as gelatin; if unavailable, use
   lemon extract)

Line an 8-inch square baking pan with plastic wrap; set aside. In a 1-quart saucepan, combine cream and gelatin. Stir with a wooden spoon until well-mixed. Place over low heat and stir constantly until mixture begins to steam; *do not allow it to boil*. Remove from heat and cool to lukewarm. Place melted coating in a medium-size bowl. Add cream mixture and extract. Using electric mixer, beat until well-blended. Refrigerate for 5 minutes. Remove from refrigerator and beat for 2 minutes. Spoon into prepared pan. Refrigerate 2 hours or until firm. Cut into 1-inch squares. Store in refrigerator. Makes 64 pieces.

Note: To form truffles into balls, see note on page 47.

Lemon Soufflé Truffles

Light, airy and delicious.

2/3 cup whipping cream
1-1/3 pounds (about 3-1/4 cups) yellow
   compound coating, melted

1 teaspoon lemon extract
1/2 teaspoon citric acid

Line an 8-inch square baking pan with plastic wrap; set aside. In a 1-quart saucepan, scald cream. Cool until a drop feels very warm on the wrist. Stir in extract and citric acid. Place melted coating in a medium-size bowl. Pour cream mixture over top. Using electric mixer, beat until thoroughly blended. Refrigerate for 5 minutes. Remove from refrigerator and beat for 2 minutes or until mixture is fluffy. Spoon into prepared pan. Refrigerate 2 hours or until firm. Cut into 1-inch squares and serve immediately. Store in refrigerator. Makes 81 pieces.

Note: To form truffles into balls, see note on page 47.

Variations
Sprinkle top with 1/2 cup coconut.
Use orange coating in place of yellow, and orange extract in place of lemon.
Use white coating, and add 1/2 cup chopped candied cherries, 1/2 cup roasted unsalted almonds and 1/2 teaspoon almond extract.

Economy Mint Truffles

Less expensive than the preceding recipes—but nonetheless delicious.

**1-1/2 pounds (about 4-1/2 cups)
  chocolate-flavored compound coating,
  melted**

**3/4 cup evaporated milk
4 drops oil of peppermint**

Line an 8-inch square baking pan with plastic wrap; set aside. Place melted compound coating in a medium-size bowl; set aside. Pour evaporated milk into a 1-quart saucepan. Place over medium heat and bring to a simmer; do not allow it to boil. Remove from heat and let stand 5 minutes. Add oil of peppermint. Pour over coating. Using electric mixer, beat until mixture is smooth and thick. Pour into prepared pan. Refrigerate 2 hours or until firm. Cut into 1-inch squares and serve immediately. Store in refrigerator. Makes 64 pieces.

Note: To form truffles into balls, see note on page 47.

Economy Bavarian Mints

Similar to truffles, but not as rich.

**1-1/2 pounds (about 4-1/2 cups) milk
  chocolate (either dipping chocolate or
  chocolate pieces), melted**

**3/4 cup evaporated milk
1/4 cup margarine
1/2 teaspoon peppermint extract**

Line an 8-inch square baking pan with plastic wrap; set aside. Place melted chocolate in a medium-size bowl. Combine evaporated milk and margarine in a 1-quart saucepan. Place over medium heat until margarine is melted. Remove from heat. Add extract. Allow to stand 5 minutes. Pour milk mixture over chocolate. Using electric mixer, beat until well-blended and thick. Pour into prepared pan. Refrigerate overnight. Cut into 1-inch squares and serve immediately. Store in refrigerator. Makes 64 pieces.

Note: To form into balls, see note on page 47.

Bavarian Mints

Use chocolate pieces if you don't have dipping chocolate. This recipe cannot fail.

1 pound (about 3 cups) dipping chocolate *or*
  2-1/2 cups chocolate pieces
1 (1-ounce) square unsweetened baking
  chocolate

1 (14-ounce) can sweetened condensed milk
4 drops oil of peppermint

Line an 8-inch square baking pan with plastic wrap; set aside. Melt dipping and baking chocolates together. Place in a medium-size bowl. Pour milk over chocolate; add oil of peppermint. Using electric mixer, beat until well-blended. Pour into prepared pan. Refrigerate 2 hours or until firm. Cut into 1-inch squares and serve immediately. Store in refrigerator. Makes 64 pieces.

Note: To form into balls, see note on page 47.

Quick Penouche

The easiest, best-tasting penouche you'll ever make.

2 cups whipping cream
1 tablespoon light corn syrup
2 cups granulated sugar
1 cup firmly packed brown sugar
3 tablespoons butter

1/2 cup (2 to 3 ounces) white compound
  coating
1-1/2 cups pecans, toasted, if desired (see
  page 17)

Line an 8-inch square baking pan with plastic wrap; set aside. In a heavy 4-quart saucepan, combine cream, corn syrup and sugars. Place over medium heat and stir with a wooden spoon until mixture comes to a boil. If sugar crystals are present, wash down sides of the pan with a wet pastry brush.

Clip on thermometer. Cook, stirring occasionally, to 236F (115C) or soft-ball stage. Remove from heat. Without stirring, add butter. Let stand until thermometer cools to 210F (100C). Without stirring, add compound coating. Let stand 1 minute. Remove thermometer. Add nuts and stir with a wooden spoon until coating is melted and butter is incorporated. Candy should be thick and creamy. Scrape into prepared pan. Refrigerate 3 hours or until firm. Cut into 1-inch squares. Store in refrigerator. Makes 64 pieces.

Holiday Fudge

Use your favorite combination of nuts and fruits. Serve "plain" or dip individual pieces in melted chocolate.

1-1/2 cups whipping cream
1 cup light corn syrup
1/4 cup butter
3 cups sugar
1 teaspoon vanilla
1 cup Brazil nuts

1 cup pecans
1 cup walnuts
1 cup red or green candied cherries
1 cup candied pineapple chunks
Tempered dipping chocolate (pages
 146-153), if desired

Butter a 9" x 13" baking pan; set aside. In a heavy 4-quart saucepan, combine cream, corn syrup, butter and sugar. Place over medium heat and stir occasionally with a wooden spoon until mixture comes to a boil. If sugar crystals are present, wash down sides of the pan with a wet pastry brush.

Clip on candy thermometer. Cook to 238F (115C) or soft-ball stage. Remove from heat and let stand undisturbed until thermometer reads 200F (95C). Remove thermometer. With a wooden spoon, beat mixture until it thickens and lightens in color. Stir in vanilla, nuts and fruits and mix well. Turn into prepared pan, pressing mixture into corners. Refrigerate 24 hours. Cut into 1-inch squares and serve, or dip in chocolate. Makes 117 pieces.

No-Beat Chocolate Fudge

A popular marshmallow-chocolate fudge.

1 (12-ounce) package semisweet chocolate
 pieces
1 (7-ounce) jar marshmallow creme
1 (12-ounce) can evaporated milk

1/2 cup butter or margarine
4 cups sugar
2 cups coarsely chopped nuts, if desired

Butter a 9" x 13" baking pan; set aside. Combine chocolate pieces and marshmallow creme in a large bowl; set aside. In a heavy 4-quart saucepan, combine milk, butter and sugar. Place over medium heat and stir occasionally with a wooden spoon until mixture comes to a boil. Boil, stirring occasionally, for 6 minutes.

Pour over chocolate-marshmallow creme mixture. Using a wooden spoon, beat until mixture is creamy. Stir in nuts. Pour fudge into prepared pan. Refrigerate 6 hours or until firm. Cut into 1-inch squares. Keeps well for several weeks in the refrigerator. Makes 117 pieces.

Variation
For Rocky Road Fudge—Add 2 cups miniature marshmallows along with nuts.

Holiday Fudge and Rocky Road Fudge lead to a plate of assorted truffles (pages 46-50).

Golden Fudge

Start a tradition of making this delightful fudge at Christmas time.

1 cup evaporated milk or whipping cream	3 cups sugar
1/2 cup water	1/2 teaspoon salt
1/4 cup light corn syrup	1 teaspoon vanilla
3 tablespoons butter	

Butter an 8-inch square baking pan; set aside. In a heavy 4-quart saucepan, combine milk, water, corn syrup, butter, sugar and salt. Place over medium-high heat and stir with a wooden spoon until mixture comes to a boil. If sugar crystals are present, wash down sides of pan with a wet pastry brush.

Clip on candy thermometer. Stirring constantly, cook to 238F (115C) or soft-ball stage. Remove from heat. Without stirring, pour vanilla over mixture. Leaving thermometer in the pan, cool mixture to 110F (45C). Remove thermometer. Using wooden spoon, stir mixture for several minutes until it starts to thicken and lose its gloss. Scrape into prepared pan. Refrigerate 4 hours or until firm. Cut into 1-inch squares. Makes 64 pieces.

Variations

For Cherry Fudge—Cut 32 candied cherries in half. Mark fudge into 1-inch pieces. While fudge is still warm, place 1 cherry half on top of each piece.

For Nut Fudge—Stir in 1 cup walnuts, pecans or peanuts before pouring fudge into pan.

For Cherry Nut Fudge—Stir in 1/2 cup chopped candied cherries and 1/2 cup unsalted nuts before pouring fudge into pan.

For Coconut Fudge—Stir in 3/4 cup coconut before pouring fudge into pan.

For Pineapple-Coconut Fudge—Stir in 1/3 cup chopped candied pineapple, 1/2 teaspoon pineapple extract and 1/2 cup coconut before pouring fudge into pan.

For Lemon or Orange Fudge—Stir in 1 teaspoon lemon or orange extract and 4 drops food color before pouring fudge into pan.

Maggie's No-Fail Chocolate Fudge

A long-time caterer's favorite candy, this no-cook fudge has a terrific taste! Use a glass dish or line a metal pan with plastic wrap as this candy will pick up the taste of the metal from the pan.

1 (8-ounce) package semisweet chocolate squares
1/2 cup margarine
2 eggs

1 (1-pound) box powdered sugar
1 teaspoon vanilla
1 cup whole nuts

Butter a 9-inch square glass baking dish; set aside. In a 1-quart saucepan, combine chocolate and margarine. Place over low heat and stir occasionally until melted. Cool to lukewarm. In a medium-size bowl, beat eggs with an electric mixer. Add powdered sugar and vanilla and blend well. Beat in chocolate mixture. Stir in nuts. Turn into prepared dish. Refrigerate 2 hours or until firm. To serve, cut into 1-inch squares. Store in refrigerator. Makes 81 pieces.

Irene's Tutti-Frutti Fudge

Fruits and nuts make this candy a hit.

1/4 cup unsweetened cocoa
1 (14-ounce) can sweetened condensed milk
1 cup water
2 tablespoon finely grated orange peel
1 tablespoon light corn syrup

4 cups granulated sugar
1 cup firmly packed brown sugar
1 cup chopped dates
1 cup chopped nuts

In a heavy 4-quart saucepan, combine cocoa, condensed milk, water, orange peel, corn syrup and sugars. Place over medium heat and stir with a wooden spoon until mixture comes to a boil. If sugar crystals are present, wash down sides of pan with a wet pastry brush.

Clip on candy thermometer. Cook to 236F (115C) or soft-ball stage. Remove from heat and allow mixture to cool to lukewarm.

Meanwhile, butter a 9-inch square baking pan; set aside. Add dates and nuts to fudge. Using a wooden spoon, stir until mixture thickens and begins to set up. Scrape into prepared pan. Refrigerate 3 hours or until firm. Cut into 1-inch squares. Serve immediately, or store in an airtight container in refrigerator. Makes 81 pieces.

Quick Chocolate Fudge

This also makes an excellent frosting—sufficient to generously cover a 9" x 13" sheet cake.

1/2 cup evaporated milk
1/4 cup margarine
1-1/2 cups sugar
20 large marshmallows

1 (6-ounce) package semisweet chocolate
   pieces
1/2 teaspoon vanilla

Butter an 8-inch square baking pan; set aside. In a heavy 2-quart saucepan, combine milk, margarine and sugar. Place over medium-high heat and stir constantly with a wooden spoon until mixture comes to a boil. Boil for 5 minutes. Remove from heat. Use a clean wooden spoon to stir in marshmallows, chocolate and vanilla. Stir until melted. Pour into prepared pan. Refrigerate 3 hours or until firm. Cut into 1-inch squares. Store in refrigerator. Makes 64 pieces.

Variations
Add 1/2 cup chopped nuts along with marshmallows.
For Quick Chocolate Fudge Frosting—Boil mixture for only 3 minutes. Remove from heat. Add marshmallows, chocolate pieces and vanilla and stir until melted. Allow to stand in saucepan until mixture holds its shape, stirring occasionally. If mixture is too thick, add hot water 1 tablespoon at a time until frosting reaches spreading consistency. Spread on cake.

Buttermilk Fudge

Commercial buttermilk gives this fudge a delicious tang.

1 cup buttermilk
1/2 cup margarine
3 tablespoons light corn syrup
1 teaspoon baking soda

2 cups sugar
1 teaspoon vanilla
2 cups nuts, if desired

Butter a 9-inch square baking pan; set aside. In a heavy 2-quart saucepan, combine buttermilk, margarine, corn syrup, baking soda and sugar. Place over medium-high heat and stir occasionally with a wooden spoon until mixture comes to a boil. If sugar crystals are present, wash down sides of pan with a wet pastry brush.

   Clip on candy thermometer. Stirring constantly, cook to 236F (115C) or soft-ball stage. Remove from heat. Leave thermometer and wooden spoon in pan and let mixture stand undisturbed until temperature cools to 210F (100C). Add vanilla and nuts and stir until mixture is creamy. Pour into prepared pan. Refrigerate 3 hours or until firm. Cut into 1-inch squares. Store in refrigerator. Makes 81 pieces.

Peanut Butter Fudge

A favorite of the kids. Rolled into balls, this fudge also makes an excellent center for chocolates.

1-1/4 cups milk
1/4 cup light corn syrup
1/4 cup margarine
Pinch of baking soda
3 cups granulated sugar

1 cup lightly packed brown sugar
3/4 cup creamy or chunky peanut butter
1 teaspoon vanilla
1 cup coarsely chopped peanuts, if desired

Set aside a 9" x 13" ungreased baking pan. Cover a baking sheet with waxed paper; set aside. In a heavy 4-quart saucepan, combine milk, corn syrup, margarine, baking soda and sugars. Place over medium-high heat and stir occasionally with a wooden spoon until mixture comes to a boil. If sugar crystals are present, wash down sides of pan with a wet pastry brush.

Clip on candy thermometer. Stirring constantly, cook to 234F (110C) or soft-ball stage. Pour without scraping into baking pan. Cool until bottom of pan feels warm but not hot. Using a wooden spoon, stir in peanut butter, vanilla and nuts. Continue stirring until mixture becomes creamy and begins to lose its gloss. Scrape fudge onto the sheet of waxed paper and spread 1 inch thick. When firm, cut into 1-inch squares. Store in refrigerator. Makes about 75 pieces.

Virginia Fudge

Brown sugar gives this candy its distinctive flavor.

1 (12-ounce) can evaporated milk
1/2 cup butter
2 tablespoons light corn syrup
2 cups firmly packed brown sugar

1 cup granulated sugar
1 teaspoon vanilla
2 cups pecans

Set aside an ungreased 9" x 13" baking pan. In a heavy 4-quart saucepan, combine milk, butter, corn syrup and sugars. Place over medium heat and stir occasionally with a wooden spoon until mixture comes to a boil. If sugar crystals are present, wash down sides of the pan with a wet pastry brush.

Clip on candy thermometer. Cook to 234F (115C) or soft-ball stage. Pour without scraping into baking pan. Cool until lukewarm. Add vanilla. Stir with a wooden spoon until mixture thickens. Add nuts and continue stirring until candy loses its gloss. Scrape out onto plastic wrap. Pat into a loaf shape about 9" x 5". Slice and serve, or wrap in plastic wrap and store in the refrigerator for several weeks. Makes about 50 slices or 75 pieces.

Variation
Use 1 teaspoon maple extract in place of vanilla.

Coffee Fudge

Especially for those who enjoy the flavor of coffee.

2/3 cup liquid coffee
1/3 cup whipping cream
2 cups sugar
1/8 teaspoon salt

3 tablespoons butter
1/2 teaspoon vanilla
1/4 cup chopped nuts, if desired

In a heavy 3-quart saucepan, combine coffee, cream, sugar and salt. Place over medium heat and stir occasionally with a wooden spoon until mixture comes to a boil. If sugar crystals are present, wash down sides of pan with a wet pastry brush.

Clip on candy thermometer. Cook, stirring constantly, to 234F (110C) or soft-ball stage. Remove from heat. Without stirring, add butter and vanilla. Let stand 15 minutes. Using a wooden spoon, stir fudge until it thickens and begins to lose its gloss. If fudge hardens too much, knead with your hands to soften. Form into rolls. Slice and serve, or wrap in plastic wrap and store in refrigerator. Makes about 50 pieces.

Hot Fudge Sauce

My husband Ron's favorite. It's great served over vanilla ice cream; in fact, this is great served over almost anything! It can be reheated in the microwave or over direct low heat.

1 (12-ounce) can evaporated milk
1/2 cup butter
3 (1-ounce) squares unsweetened baking
  chocolate

2 cups sugar
1 teaspoon vanilla

In heavy 2-quart saucepan, combine milk, butter, chocolate and sugar. Place over medium heat and stir occasionally with a wooden spoon until mixture comes to a boil. Stirring constantly, boil until mixture thickens, 5 to 10 minutes. Remove from heat. Stir in vanilla. Cool sauce 20 minutes before using or it will be too hot for the ice cream. Store in the refrigerator. Makes about 2 cups.

Superb Pralines

A traditional Southern recipe.

1 cup buttermilk
1 teaspoon baking soda
2 cups sugar

3 tablespoons butter
1 teaspoon vanilla
2 cups pecans

Line a 15″ x 10″ jellyroll pan with waxed paper; set aside. In a heavy 2-quart saucepan, combine buttermilk and soda. Using a wooden spoon, stir in sugar. Place over medium heat and stir constantly until mixture comes to a boil. If sugar crystals are present, wash down sides of pan with a wet pastry brush.

Clip on candy thermometer. Continue cooking to 236F (115C) or soft-ball stage. Remove from heat and stir in butter, vanilla and pecans. Stir with a wooden spoon until mixture is creamy. Spoon onto waxed paper forming 2-inch patties. Cool at room temperature. Makes 25 patties.

Orange Pralines

An interesting combination of flavors.

1 cup whipping cream
2 tablespoons light corn syrup
3 cups sugar

Grated peel from 1 orange
2 cups pecans

Line a 15″ x 10″ jellyroll pan with waxed paper; set aside. In a heavy 4-quart saucepan, combine cream, corn syrup and sugar. Place over medium heat and stir with a wooden spoon until mixture comes to a boil. If sugar crystals are present, wash down sides of the pan with a wet pastry brush.

Clip on candy thermometer. Cook to 238F (115C) or soft-ball stage. Remove from heat and, without stirring, add orange peel. Let stand 15 minutes. Add pecans and stir until mixture thickens and begins to lose its gloss. Spoon onto waxed paper forming 2-inch patties. Makes about 40 patties.

A collection of delicious caramels, clockwise from top right, they are Divinity Dips (page 70), Golden Caramels (page 64), Caramel Clusters (page 70), Caramel-Nougat Pinwheels (page 80) and Pecan Logs (page 70).

Caramels

Soft, tender and golden brown—caramels rank high on the list of favorite candies. There are many variations of caramel, from cut caramels, caramel apples and pecan logs to caramel clusters, and they are all delicious.

Caramel is usually made from white or brown sugar, corn syrup, milk and/or cream.

The proportion of corn syrup to sugar determines the texture of the finished caramel. The more corn syrup in the recipe, the tougher the caramel will be.

Caramels should be cooked slowly to allow the sugars and milk solids to caramelize. The longer and slower they are cooked, the darker the color and stronger the flavor. The faster they are cooked, the lighter the color and flavor. It is important not to cook caramels too fast or they will scorch and have an unpleasant burnt flavor.

Many of our caramel recipes call for adding part of the liquids at the beginning of the cooking, then adding the rest later. This is called "slacking back the batch." There are two reasons for this technique: to prevent the caramel mixture from boiling over the pan, and to develop a smoother texture.

Occasionally, the caramel mixture will curdle while cooking. This is due to an excess of acid reacting with the milk. This can be avoided by making sure the mixture boils continually, or it can be eliminated by the addition of a pinch of baking soda stirred in while the mixture is cooking.

When the caramel has reached the correct temperature, it will become thick and golden and require constant stirring. If you get busy and notice the temperature of the caramels has gone higher than desired, add 1/2 cup of hot water and stir until the mixture is smooth. This will drop the temperature of the caramels. Then just continue cooking to the proper temperature.

Some of our recipes call for brown sugar or dark corn syrup. This will shorten the cooking time by adding the stronger flavor and darker color, without waiting for the cooking to develop it.

When pouring out the batch, do not scrape the excess caramel left in the cooking pan into the cooling pan. Instead, scrape it into a buttered dish and eat it separately. Scraping won't cause crystallization as it does in fondants, but the last bit in the cooking pan usually is cooked longer, is tougher and will leave hard spots in the poured-out batch.

If possible, allow caramels to stand for 24 hours before cutting. This makes them less sticky and easier to cut.

Store caramels in a cool place, not the refrigerator. Caramels absorb moisture from the air and a refrigerator has a lot of moisture in it. Cut and wrap in squares of plastic wrap or waxed paper, or cover the entire batch with plastic wrap and store where it is cool. If caramels flatten at room temperature, press them into shape with your fingers.

CARAMEL TIPS

If you want to make one batch of caramels but want nuts in only part of the candy, place nuts in only one side of the cooling pan and pour the hot caramel over them. Half of the caramels will contain nuts and half will be plain.

If your caramels are undercooked, you can recook them by adding 1-1/2 cups hot water and recooking to the proper temperature. You can also thin the candy with a little cream, and use it as an ice cream topping.

Caramels can scorch easily if not stirred during the last of the cooking period.

30-Minute Caramels

My teenager, Jeff, thinks these are the greatest.

1 (14-ounce) can sweetened condensed milk	**1/2 cup butter**
1-1/2 cups light corn syrup	**1/4 teaspoon salt**
1 cup granulated sugar	**Tempered dipping chocolate (pages**
1 cup firmly packed brown sugar	**146-153), if desired**

Butter a 9-inch square baking pan; set aside. In a heavy 4-quart saucepan, combine milk, corn syrup, sugars, butter and salt. Place over medium heat and stir with a wooden spoon until mixture comes to a boil.

Clip on candy thermometer. Stirring constantly to prevent scorching, cook to 240F (115C) or soft-ball stage. Pour into prepared pan. Cool at room temperature until firm. Cut into 1-inch squares. Wrap in waxed paper or dip in tempered chocolate. Makes 81 pieces.

Variation
Add 1 cup nuts (roasted cashews are especially good) before pouring into cooling pan.

Shirley's Wonderful Caramels

These taste so good, everyone will ask for this recipe. If you don't happen to have a 6-quart pan, cut the recipe in half and pour the caramels into a 9-inch square pan.

2 cups light corn syrup
1 (14-ounce) can sweetened condensed milk
1-1/2 cups milk
1 cup whipping cream
1 cup butter
4 cups sugar
2 teaspoons vanilla
2 cups nuts
Tempered dipping chocolate (pages 146-153), if desired

Butter a 9" x 13" baking pan; set aside. In a heavy 6-quart Dutch oven, combine corn syrup, condensed milk, milk, cream, butter and sugar. Place over medium heat and stir occasionally with a wooden spoon until mixture comes to a boil. If sugar crystals are present, wash down sides of pan with a wet pastry brush.

Clip on candy thermometer. Cook, stirring constantly, to 240F (115C) or soft-ball stage. Remove from heat. Stir in vanilla and nuts. Pour without scraping into prepared pan. Allow to stand at room temperature overnight. Cut into about 1-inch rectangles or squares. Wrap in waxed paper or dip in tempered chocolate. Makes 117 pieces.

CUTTING & WRAPPING CARAMELS

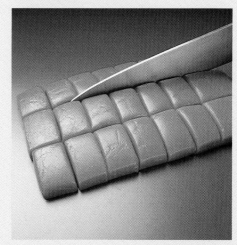

Caramels will be less sticky and easier to cut if you can resist temptation and wait 24 hours after they are cooked. A heavy, sharp knife or metal pastry scraper does a neat job—easily and efficiently.

Cut caramels can either be wrapped with plastic wrap or waxed paper, or the entire pan can be overwrapped, stored in a cool area—but not the refrigerator—and caramels can be cut to order.

Golden Caramels

Our favorite all-around caramel.

2 cups whipping cream
1/2 cup milk
1-1/4 cups light corn syrup
2 cups sugar
1/4 teaspoon salt

1/2 cup evaporated milk
1 teaspoon vanilla
Tempered dipping chocolate (pages
    146-153), if desired

Butter an 8-inch square baking pan; set aside. In a 4-cup glass measure or small bowl, combine cream and milk. In a heavy 4-quart saucepan, combine 1/3 of the cream-milk mixture, corn syrup, sugar and salt. Place over low heat and stir occasionally with a wooden spoon until mixture comes to a boil. Boil, stirring occasionally, for 30 minutes, or until mixture turns a light tan color.

Clip on candy thermometer. Increase heat to medium. Without stopping the boiling action, slowly pour in 1/2 of the remaining cream-milk mixture. Stirring constantly, cook for 15 minutes. Slowly pour in the remaining cream-milk mixture and the evaporated milk. When temperature reaches 242F (120C) or firm-ball, remove from heat and stir in vanilla. Without scraping, pour mixture into prepared pan. Allow to stand at room temperature overnight. Cut into 1-inch squares. Dip each piece in tempered chocolate, if desired, or wrap individually in waxed paper. Store at room temperature. Makes 64 pieces.

Variation
One cup nuts may be added with the vanilla.

Soft Caramels

These caramels will melt in your mouth—and they won't stick in your teeth!

2 cups whipping cream
1/2 cup sweetened condensed milk
2 cups light corn syrup
1/2 cup water

2 cups sugar
1/2 cup butter
Tempered dipping chocolate (pages
    146-153), if desired

Butter a 9-inch square baking pan; set aside. In a 1-quart saucepan, combine cream and milk. Place over low heat and let warm but do not allow to boil while cooking sugar. In a 4-quart saucepan, combine corn syrup, water and sugar. Place over high heat and stir with a wooden spoon until well-mixed. If sugar crystals are present, wash down sides of the pan with a wet pastry brush.

Clip on candy thermometer. Reduce heat to medium. Bring to a boil and cook to 250F (120C) or hard-ball stage. Stir in butter and warm cream-milk mixture. Temperature will decrease. Stirring constantly, continue cooking over medium heat until thermometer reaches 244F (120C) or firm-ball stage. Pour into prepared pan. Cool overnight. Cut in 1-inch squares. Wrap in waxed paper or dip in tempered chocolate. Makes 81 pieces.

Orange Caramels

Cashew pieces are especially good in this unusual caramel.

1 cup light corn syrup
1 (6-ounce) can frozen orange juice
  concentrate, thawed
2 cups sugar

1/4 teaspoon salt
1 cup whipping cream
1/2 cup butter, cut in pieces
2 cups nuts, if desired

Butter an 8-inch square baking pan; set aside. In a heavy 4-quart saucepan, combine corn syrup, orange juice concentrate, sugar and salt. Place over medium heat and stir with a wooden spoon until well-mixed. If sugar crystals are present, wash down sides of pan with a wet pastry brush.

Clip on candy thermometer. Cook, stirring constantly, to 248F (120C) or firm-ball stage. Stir in cream and butter. Temperature will decrease. Cook to 245F (120C) or firm-ball. Remove from heat and stir in nuts. Pour into prepared pan. Allow to stand at room temperature overnight. Cut into 1-inch squares. Wrap in waxed paper or plastic wrap. Makes 64 pieces.

Licorice Caramels

Black, chewy and delicious. Paste food colors are available from cake decorating suppliers.

1 (14-ounce) can sweetened condensed milk
1-1/2 cups corn syrup
1 cup butter or margarine
2 cups sugar

1/4 teaspoon salt
2 teaspoons anise oil (check supplier list on
  page 155)
1 teaspoon black paste food color

Butter a 9-inch square baking pan; set aside. In a heavy 4-quart saucepan, combine condensed milk, corn syrup, butter, sugar and salt. Place over medium heat and stir with a wooden spoon until well-mixed. If sugar crystals are present, wash down sides of pan with a wet pastry brush.

Clip on candy thermometer. Cook, stirring constantly, to 242F (120C) or firm-ball stage. Remove from heat and stir in flavoring and food color; blend well. Without scraping, pour into prepared pan. Allow to stand at room temperature overnight. Cut into 1-inch squares. Wrap in waxed paper or plastic wrap. Makes 81 pieces.

Variation
For Red Licorice Caramels—Use 2 teaspoons wild cherry oil and 1 teaspoon red paste food color.

Naomi's Fudgy Caramels

A delightful cross between fudge and caramel.

2 cups whipping cream
1 cup milk
3/4 cup light corn syrup
2 cups sugar
1/4 teaspoon salt

1/2 teaspoon vanilla
1 cup chopped nuts
Tempered dipping chocolate (pages
   146-153), if desired

Butter a 9-inch square baking pan; set aside. In a heavy 4-quart saucepan, combine cream, milk, corn syrup, sugar and salt. Place over low heat and cook, stirring occasionally with a wooden spoon, until mixture is a light tan color, 20 to 30 minutes. If sugar crystals are present, wash down sides of pan with a wet pastry brush.

Clip on candy thermometer. Cook, stirring occasionally, to 238F (115C) or soft-ball stage. Remove from heat. Remove thermometer. Add vanilla and nuts.

With an electric mixer on high speed, beat mixture until it turns a lighter color and is very thick, about 5 minutes. Scrape into prepared pan. Cover with plastic wrap. Let stand at room temperature for 2 days to crystallize the caramel. Cut into 1-inch squares and serve plain, or dip in tempered chocolate. Makes 81 pieces.

Dark Caramels

Strong-flavored caramels with a dark color.

2 pounds (about 8 cups) pecan pieces or
   halves
4 cups (2 pints) whipping cream, divided
2 cups dark corn syrup
2-1/4 cups firmly packed brown sugar

2-1/4 cups granulated sugar
3/4 pound (1-1/2 cups) butter
Tempered dipping chocolate (pages
   146-153), if desired

Butter a 9" X 13" baking pan. Cover bottom with pecans; set aside. In a heavy 4-quart saucepan, combine 2 cups of the cream, corn syrup, sugars and butter. Place over medium heat and stir with a wooden spoon until well-blended. If sugar crystals are present, wash down sides of pan with a wet pastry brush.

Clip on candy thermometer. Cook, stirring gently, to 240F (115C) or soft-ball stage. Increase heat to medium-high. Stirring gently but constantly, add remaining 2 cups of cream in a slow trickle. When all the cream has been added, reduce heat to medium and continue stirring until syrup reaches 240F (115C) or soft-ball stage. If the temperature goes higher than this, stir in 1/4 cup hot water; this will reduce the temperature and allow you to cook to the proper temperature again. When proper temperature is reached, pour caramels into prepared pan. Let cool overnight. Cut into 1-inch squares and served plain, or dip in chocolate. Makes 117 pieces.

Chocolate Caramels

My son Ryan's favorite treat.

2 cups whipping cream, divided
1-1/2 cups light corn syrup
2 cups sugar
1/4 teaspoon salt

3 (1-ounce) squares unsweetened baking
   chocolate
1/2 cup butter
Tempered dipping chocolate (pages
   146-153), if desired

Butter a 9-inch square baking pan; set aside. In a heavy 4-quart saucepan, combine 1 cup of the cream, corn syrup, sugar and salt. Place over medium heat and stir occasionally with a wooden spoon until mixture comes to a boil. If sugar crystals are present, wash down sides of pan with a wet pastry brush.

   Clip on candy thermometer. Cook, stirring occasionally, until temperature reaches 220F (105C). Add chocolate and butter and stir constantly for the remainder of the cooking time. Without allowing boil to stop, slowly pour in remaining 1 cup cream. Cook to 240F (115C) or soft-ball stage. Without scraping, pour into prepared pan. Allow to stand at room temperature overnight. To serve, cut into 1-inch squares. Wrap individually in waxed paper, or dip in tempered chocolate. Store at room temperature. Makes 81 pieces.

Variation
Stir in 1 cup nuts before pouring caramels into cooling pan.

Peanut Caramel

Use this alone, or in our Snicks recipe on page 83.

1 cup light corn syrup
1 cup whipping cream
1/2 cup milk

1-1/2 cups sugar
1/4 teaspoon salt
2 cups peanuts

Butter a 9-inch square baking pan; set aside. In a heavy 4-quart saucepan, combine corn syrup, cream, milk, sugar and salt. Place over medium heat and stir occasionally with a wooden spoon until mixture comes to a boil. If any sugar crystals are present, wash down sides of pan with wet pastry brush.

   Clip on candy thermometer. Cook, stirring occasionally, to 240F (115C) or soft-ball stage. Remove from heat and stir in peanuts. Pour into prepared pan, scraping sides with wooden spoon. Let stand at room temperature until cool. Cut into 1-inch pieces. Makes 81 pieces.

Variation
When using Peanut Caramel for Snicks, pour into a buttered 15″ x 10″ jellyroll pan. Cut into pieces about 1″ x 2″. Makes about 55 bars.

Pecan Rolls

This recipe resembles Pecan Logs (page 70), but the method used here results in a heavier layer of caramel. (These proportions also give a caramel that is less sticky than most.)

2-1/2 pounds (about 10 cups) pecan pieces or
  halves
1/4 cup butter, melted
1/4 cup all-purpose flour
2 cups whipping cream
1/2 cup milk

1 cup light corn syrup
2 cups sugar
1/4 teaspoon salt
1/2 recipe Cream Fondant flavored with 1
  teaspoon maple or rum extract (page 24)

Butter a 15" x 10" jellyroll pan. Spread pecans evenly over bottom, making a thick layer; set aside. In a small bowl, combine melted butter and flour; set aside.

In a 4-cup measure or small bowl, combine cream and milk. In a heavy 4-quart saucepan, combine 1/2 of the cream-milk mixture with corn syrup, sugar and salt. Place over low heat and stir with a wooden spoon until mixture comes to a boil. If any sugar crystals are present, wash down sides of pan with a wet pastry brush. Boil slowly for 30 minutes.

Clip on candy thermometer. Increase heat to medium and, stirring constantly, slowly pour in remaining cream-milk mixture; mixture should not be allowed to stop boiling. Stir in butter-flour mixture. When temperature reaches 242F (120C) or firm-ball stage, pour without scraping over pecans. Spread smooth with a spatula. Allow to cool at room temperature until caramel is warm to the touch.

Cut caramel into 12 pieces approximately 3" X 4"; remove from pan using pancake turner and place nut-side-down on waxed paper. Press slightly to flatten.

Form fondant into logs approximately 1/2" x 3". Place log of fondant in the center of flattened caramel. Wrap caramel around fondant, pressing edges and ends of caramel together to seal; roll smooth between your hands. Wrap in plastic wrap and place in refrigerator to prevent roll from flattening. To serve, let candy warm to room temperature and slice in rounds 1/2 inch thick. Makes 12 4-inch rolls.

Variations

Use Daphne's Divinity (page 77) instead of fondant.
Add cut-up candied cherries to Daphne's Divinity and use for the centers.
Use Brown Sugar Fondant flavored with maple or rum extract (page 40).
Try a combination of 1/2 Daphne's Divinity (page 77) and 1/2 Cream Fondant (page 24) kneaded together for centers.

Dipping Caramel

This recipe can be used for a number of candies. Directions for six delicious variations follow.

2 cups light corn syrup	**Pinch of baking soda**
1/2 cup water	**1/2 cup butter**
2 cups sugar	**1 (12-ounce) can evaporated milk**

In a heavy 4-quart saucepan, combine corn syrup, water and sugar. Place over medium heat and stir occasionally with a wooden spoon until mixture comes to a boil. Add soda and stir well. If sugar crystals are present, wash down sides of pan with a wet pastry brush.

Clip on candy thermometer. Add butter and stir until thoroughly incorporated. Stirring constantly and without allowing mixture to stop boiling, slowly add milk. Continue cooking over medium heat, stirring constantly to keep mixture from scorching. When temperature reaches 242F (120C) or firm-ball stage, remove from heat and allow caramel to cool to 200F (95C). Use to dip the following candies; if caramel cools too much to use in recipes, reheat over low heat.

Variations

For Pecan Logs—(This recipe is similar in flavor and appearance to Pecan Rolls on page 69. This method uses less caramel and gives a more uniform, rounder roll.) Form Cream Fondant flavored with 1 tablespoon vanilla, maple or rum extract (page 24) into logs about 1" x 3". Place logs on waxed paper-lined tray. Freeze overnight. Using a 2-tined fork, dip each frozen fondant log into warm Dipping Caramel, then onto a bed of pecan pieces or halves. Cover the caramel completely with nuts, pressing gently so nuts adhere to caramel. Place log on waxed paper to cool. Repeat with remaining logs. When candies are cold, cover tightly with plastic wrap and store in refrigerator or other cool area. Makes 10 logs.

For Divinity Dips—Form Daphne's Divinity (page 77) into 1-inch balls. Using a 2-tined fork, dip divinity in warm Dipping Caramel, coating completely, or, by hand, dip top half of divinity in caramel. Roll or dip in chopped nuts or coconut. Makes about 50 pieces.

For Caramel Marshmallows—Purchase large, fresh commercial marshmallows. Using a 2-tined fork, dip marshmallows 1 at a time in warm Dipping Caramel. Arrange on plastic wrap to cool. Makes enough caramel to cover about 50 marshmallows.

For Caramel Apples—Wash and dry 8 crisp apples. Insert a wooden stick about 1-1/2 inches into each stem. Dip each apple in warm caramel, turning to coat thoroughly. Place on plastic wrap or on a layer of chopped nuts.

For Caramel Clusters (Method 1)—Spread 8 cups (about 2 pounds) pecans pieces or halves in a 15" x 10" jellyroll pan, making a very thick layer. For each cluster, spoon 1 scant tablespoon warm Dipping Caramel over nuts to form patties about 1 inch in diameter; for greatest efficiency, form patties in rows as evenly as possible. If the caramel sinks to the bottom of the nuts, the caramel is too warm; allow it to cool longer. When caramel is set, use spatula or fingers to lift clusters from nuts and transfer to waxed paper-lined baking sheet. Make additional clusters, adding pecans as needed. When the caramel patties are cool to the touch, cover caramel with tempered dipping chocolate (pages 146-153), or dip entire cluster in chocolate. Makes about 60 clusters.

For Caramel Clusters (Method 2)—Arrange 4 pecan halves small end out in a "4-petal" group on a well-buttered baking sheet. Repeat to make 60 groups of nuts. Spoon 1 tablespoon warm caramel over each group of pecans. When cool to the touch, either cover caramel with tempered dipping chocolate (pages 146-153), or dip entire cluster in chocolate. Makes about 60 clusters.

Pecan Logs (page 70): Frozen logs of fondant, held by a dipping fork, are dunked into warm Dipping Caramel.

Caramel-coated fondant is dropped onto a bed of pecans and turned to cover completely. Pecans are pressed gently into caramel and set on waxed paper-lined tray.

Pecan Rolls (page 69): Warm caramel is poured as evenly as possible over a thick layer of pecans, then cut while still warm into about 3″ x 4″ rectangles.

Pecan Logs (continued): The rectangles are pressed slightly to flatten, then wrapped around fondant logs to encase completely. Additional pecan halves can be added for decoration.

Caramel Clusters/Method 1 (page 70): This is the faster method, though the finished clusters are less precise. Dipping Caramel is spooned in even rows over a thick layer of pecans. When the caramel is set, the clusters are lifted off with a metal spatula or fingers. Additional caramel can be spooned over subsequent layers until the pecans run out. To dip, see photograph on page 152.

Caramel Clusters/Method 2 (page 70): This method makes very orderly clusters. It might be preferred when more uniform results are desired (or by people with more time and patience). Pecan halves are neatly arranged in "4-petal" groups on a buttered baking sheet and a tablespoon of warm Dipping Caramel holds them together. Both versions taste the same: Delicious!

Caramel Ice Cream Topping

Tastes great hot or cold.

1 cup whipping cream
1 cup light corn syrup
1 cup sugar

1/4 teaspoon salt
1/2 teaspoon vanilla

In a heavy 2-quart saucepan, combine cream, corn syrup, sugar and salt. Place over medium heat and stir occasionally with a wooden spoon until mixture comes to a boil. If any sugar crystals are present, wash down sides of pan with a wet pastry brush.

Clip on candy thermometer. Reduce heat to maintain a slow boil. Stirring occasionally to prevent scorching, cook for at least 30 minutes to caramelize the sugar. Continue cooking to 234F (110C) or soft-ball stage. If the temperature goes higher than this before the topping is golden-brown, add 1/4 cup hot water and continue cooking; the addition of the water will reduce the temperature and allow the mixture to caramelize longer.

When the mixture is a golden-brown and has reached the proper temperature, remove from heat and stir in vanilla. Serve hot, or allow topping to cool in saucepan. If topping thickens too much when cool, stir in 1 tablespoon hot water. Topping may be stored in refrigerator for 2 weeks. Reheat in the microwave or in a small saucepan over low heat, or serve cold. Makes about 2 cups.

Baked Caramel Corn

An easy recipe for caramel corn the whole family will love!

6 quarts unbuttered, unsalted popped
  popcorn
1 cup peanuts, if desired
1 cup butter or margarine
1/2 cup light corn syrup

2 cups firmly packed brown sugar
1 teaspoon salt
1/4 teaspoon cream of tartar
1 teaspoon baking soda

Preheat oven 200F (95C). Set two 15" x 10" jellyroll pans or a large roasting pan aside. Place popcorn and peanuts in a very large bowl. In a heavy 2-quart saucepan, combine butter, corn syrup, brown sugar, salt and cream of tartar. Place over high heat and stir with a wooden spoon until mixture comes to a boil. Stirring occasionally, let boil for 5 minutes.

Remove from heat and stir in baking soda. Immediately pour over popcorn and nuts, turning to coat each kernel. Spread mixture in pan(s) and place in oven for 1 hour, stirring every 15 minutes. Remove from oven and cool completely. Store in an airtight container to retain crispness. Makes 6 quarts.

Caramel Corn

Tastes just like the caramel corn Grandmother used to make.

4 quarts unbuttered, unsalted popped
  popcorn
1/4 cup water
3 tablespoons butter
1 tablespoon light corn syrup

1-1/2 cups firmly packed brown sugar
1/4 teaspoon salt
1/8 teaspoon baking soda

Set rimmed baking sheet aside. Place popcorn in a very large bowl; set aside. In a heavy 2-quart saucepan, combine water, butter, corn syrup, sugar and salt. Place over high heat and stir with a wooden spoon for 1 minute. Cook without stirring until mixture turns golden brown and gives off puffs of smoke (not steam). Stir and allow to smoke again. Allow to smoke a third time. Remove from heat. Add baking soda and stir well. Immediately pour over popcorn, tossing with a buttered wooden spoon or paddle to coat each kernel. Turn onto baking sheet and let stand until cooled completely. Store in an airtight container. Makes 4 quarts.

Variation
Add 1 cup peanuts or other nuts to popcorn before coating with hot syrup.

A sweet bouquet of Daphne's Divinity
(page 77); Fruit-Flavored Marshmallows
(page 82); a Marshmallow Easter Egg
decorated with piped coating and royal
icing flowers (page 81); Snicks (page
83); and foil-wrapped Marshmallow
Easter Eggs (page 81).

Divinity, Nougat & Marshmallow

Divinity, nougat and marshmallow all belong to the same candy family. Divinity is delicious by itself and very useful inasmuch as it can be combined with other candy to make really spectacular productions. You can add a little soft butter to make a white center for pecan logs or, kneaded with cream fondant, it makes a wonderful chocolate center. Coconut, nuts, fruit, chocolate and fruit-flavored gelatin may be added to give a great variety of candies.

Divinity is easy to make; just be sure you cook it to the proper temperature, remove it from the heat and let the boiling stop before pouring over the beaten egg whites. If it refuses to harden, add two tablespoons of powdered sugar and let it rest a few minutes. If it hardens too much, stir in hot water a tablespoon at a time until the desired consistency is reached.

French nougat is popular with people who like a chewy candy. It usually has nuts and candied fruit added, but it also is terrific plain. Added to a layer of caramel, rolled tightly and sliced, it makes a spectacular-looking pinwheel. Ideally, nougat—like caramels—should stand several days before cutting to improve the texture. Cut with a sharp knife and use a sawing motion.

Marshmallow is a favorite confection by itself and very useful as a candymaking ingredient. Marshmallows are good dipped in chocolate, coarsely cut and added to melted chocolate with nuts to make rocky road candy, combined with caramel to make a delicious chocolate center, or dipped in a honey glaze and rolled in toasted coconut.

The use of marshmallow creme—known as "mazetta" or "frappé"—in candy is a closely guarded confectioner's secret. Added to fondants and fudges as they are beaten, it gives a lighter, smoother texture and creamier finished product that stays fresh longer. It is also the basis for French-type nougats. Thinned with a little hot water, it makes a great ice cream topping. You can purchase marshmallow creme at the supermarket or make your own. We prefer to prepare it ourselves as it is more tender and less expensive. It doesn't take long to make and it will keep in the refrigerator for several weeks.

Cherry Nut Divinity

This delightful divinity is formed in a baking pan and cut into pieces. If you prefer, spoon it out in traditional mounds for individual servings.

2 egg whites, at room temperature
1 cup light corn syrup
3/4 cup water
3 cups sugar

1/4 teaspoon salt
1/2 cup chopped candied cherries
1 cup chopped nuts
1 teaspoon almond extract

Line a 9-inch square baking pan with plastic wrap; set aside. Place egg whites in large bowl of electric mixer; set aside. In a heavy 3-quart saucepan, combine corn syrup, water, sugar and salt. Place over low heat and stir with a wooden spoon until sugar is dissolved. Remove spoon. Increase heat to medium-high and cook without stirring until mixture reaches a rolling boil.

Clip on candy thermometer. Reduce heat to maintain full (but not rolling) boil. If sugar crystals are present, wash down sides of pan with a wet pastry brush. Cook syrup to 250F (120C) or hard-ball stage. Remove syrup from heat. Immediately begin beating egg whites at high speed until stiff peaks form. With mixer still on high speed, gradually add hot syrup to egg whites; *once you begin to pour, don't stop and do not scrape pan.* Continue beating until mixture begins to lose its gloss. Remove beaters and, using a wooden spoon, fold in cherries, nuts and extract. Scrape into prepared pan and let candy stand at room temperature to cool completely. Remove divinity from pan by lifting plastic wrap. Invert onto cutting surface, remove plastic and cut candy in 1-inch pieces. Cover tightly and store at room temperature. Makes 81 pieces.

Daphne's Divinity

A light, creamy divinity that turns out moist every time. If you prefer, use a slotted spoon or wooden paddle instead of an electric mixer for beating. Admittedly, it's easier if you have two people to take turns, but some feel the manual labor (exercise?!) is easier than trying to scrape the candy off the beaters. If you do need to rest your arms in the middle of beating, the candy will not be affected.

2 egg whites, at room temperature
1/2 cup light corn syrup
1/2 cup water
2 cups sugar
A few grains of salt
1 teaspoon vanilla
1 cup chopped walnuts, if desired

Line a 15″ x 10″ jellyroll pan with waxed paper or butter an 8-inch square pan; set aside. Place egg whites in large bowl of electric mixer; set aside. In a heavy 3-quart saucepan, combine corn syrup, water, sugar and salt. Place over low heat and stir with a wooden spoon until sugar is dissolved. Remove spoon. Increase heat to medium-high and cook without stirring until mixture reaches a rolling boil.

Clip on candy thermometer. Reduce heat to maintain full (but not rolling) boil. If sugar crystals are present, wash down sides of pan with a wet pastry brush. Cook syrup to 252F (125C) or hard-ball stage. Just before syrup is ready, beat egg whites until stiff but not dry. Remove syrup from heat and allow boiling to subside.

With mixer on high speed, gradually add hot syrup to egg whites; *once you begin to pour, don't stop and do not scrape pan.* Continue beating until mixture begins to lose its gloss and holds its shape. Add vanilla, and nuts if desired. Drop quickly by spoonfuls onto waxed paper or pour into prepared pan, spreading evenly. Makes about 40 pieces or 64 1-inch squares.

Variation
For Divinity Eggs: Scrape divinity onto waxed paper and let stand until just set. Using buttered hands, gently press divinity into buttered egg mold, *or* butter hands and form divinity into egg shapes. Remove from mold and transfer to waxed paper-lined tray. Dip divinity eggs into melted compound coating (pages 134, 146-153) or tempered dipping chocolate (pages 146-153).

Hot syrup is added in a slow steady stream to beaten egg whites. The divinity can be beaten with an electric mixer or by hand.

Divinity is properly beaten when the mixture begins to lose its gloss and will hold its shape. At this point, it is quickly spooned onto waxed paper or scraped into a buttered 8- or 9-inch square pan.

Fruit-Flavored Divinity

Try any flavor of gelatin in this delicious recipe.

2 egg whites, at room temperature
1/2 cup light corn syrup
1/2 cup water

2-1/2 cups sugar
1 (3-ounce) package fruit-flavored gelatin

Line a 15″x 10″ jellyroll pan with waxed paper; set aside. Place egg whites in large bowl of electric mixer; set aside. In a 2-quart saucepan, combine corn syrup, water and sugar. Place over high heat and stir with a wooden spoon until mixture comes to a boil. If sugar crystals are present, wash down sides of pan with a wet pastry brush.

Clip on candy thermometer. Cook to 252F (125C) or hard-ball stage. Remove from heat. Immediately beat egg whites until soft peaks form. With mixer at medium speed, gradually beat in dry gelatin. When all of gelatin has been incorporated, increase mixer speed to high and slowly add hot syrup; *once you begin to pour, don't stop.* Continue beating until mixture begins to lose its gloss and will hold its shape. Drop by teaspoons onto waxed paper. Cool completely. Store in airtight containers. Makes 50 pieces.

Seafoam Divinity

Brown sugar divinity with a light flavor.

2 egg whites, at room temperature
3/4 cup water
1/3 cup light corn syrup

1-1/2 cups sugar
1 cup firmly packed brown sugar
1 teaspoon vanilla

Line a 15″ x 10″ jellyroll pan with waxed paper; set aside. Place egg whites in large bowl of electric mixer; set aside. In a 2-quart saucepan, combine water, corn syrup and sugars. Place over high heat and stir with a wooden spoon until mixture comes to a boil. If sugar crystals are present, wash down sides of pan with a wet pastry brush.

Clip on candy thermometer. Cook to 252F (125C) or hard-ball stage. Remove from heat. Immediately beat egg whites until stiff. With mixer on high speed, slowly add hot syrup; *once you begin to pour, don't stop.* Continue beating until mixture begins to lose its gloss and will hold its shape. Stir in vanilla. Scrape entire batch onto waxed paper-lined pan or, using 2 spoons, quickly spoon candy onto waxed paper. Makes 50 pieces.

French Almond Nougat

A wonderful, chewy confection.

2-1/2 cups Mazetta (page 82)
1-1/2 cups light corn syrup
1-1/2 cups sugar
1/4 cup butter, melted
1 teaspoon vanilla

1/4 teaspoon salt
1 cup whole raw almonds
Tempered dipping chocolate (pages
  146-153), if desired

Butter a 9″ x 13″ baking pan; set aside. Place mazetta in medium-size bowl; set aside. In a 2-quart saucepan, combine corn syrup and sugar. Place over high heat and stir constantly with a wooden spoon until mixture comes to a boil. If sugar crystals are present, wash down sides of pan with a wet pastry brush.

Clip on candy thermometer. Cook to 280F (140C) or soft-crack stage. Remove from heat and let stand undisturbed for 3 minutes. Without scraping, pour entire batch into mazetta and stir with a wooden spoon until smooth. Stir in butter, vanilla and salt and mix until butter is incorporated. Fold in nuts. Pour into prepared pan. Allow to stand at room temperature until firm, 4 to 5 hours. Cut in 1-inch pieces. Wrap in plastic wrap, or dip in tempered chocolate. Makes 117 pieces.

Chewy Nougat

Terrific by itself or in Caramel-Nougat Pinwheels (page 80).

3 cups Mazetta (page 82)
1-1/2 cups light corn syrup
1-1/2 cups sugar
1/4 cup butter, melted

1 teaspoon vanilla
1/8 teaspoon salt
Tempered dipping chocolate (pages
  146-153), if desired

Butter an 8-inch square baking pan; set aside. Place mazetta in a medium-size bowl; set aside. In a 1-quart saucepan, combine corn syrup and sugar. Place over high heat and stir constantly with a wooden spoon until mixture comes to a boil. If sugar crystals are present, wash down sides of pan with a wet pastry brush.

Clip on candy thermometer. Cook to 280F (140C) or soft-crack stage. Remove from heat and let stand undisturbed for 2 minutes. Without scraping, pour entire batch into mazetta and stir with a wooden spoon until smooth. Add butter, vanilla and salt and stir with a wooden spoon until butter is incorporated. Pour into prepared pan. Allow to stand at room temperature until firm, about 3 hours. Cut and wrap in plastic wrap, or dip in tempered chocolate. Makes 64 pieces.

Pour Chewy Nougat atop a layer of Soft
Caramels, leaving about 2 inches of caramel
exposed. When set, the candy is turned
onto a counter top and rolled jellyroll-style
as tightly as possible. The rolling is
continued until the pinwheel becomes too
long to maneuver easily.

Cut the pinwheel in half and continue
rolling, again cutting in half as needed,
until the rolls are about 1 inch thick. Cut
the pinwheels in slices about 1/2 inch thick,
or wrap the rolls in plastic wrap and store
them in the refrigerator.

Caramel-Nougat Pinwheels

Chewy caramel and nougat rolled into a pinwheel.

1 recipe Soft Caramels (page 64)
1 recipe Chewy Nougat (page 79)
Tempered dipping chocolate (pages 146-153), if desired

Butter a 9″ x 13″ baking pan; set aside. Prepare Soft Caramels.
Pour into prepared pan and allow to cool at least 3 hours.

Prepare Chewy Nougat. Pour over the caramel, leaving 2
inches of caramel uncovered on one 9-inch side (this will help
the caramel stick to itself during rolling); quickly spread as
evenly as possible as nougat will begin to set up.

When nougat has set 3 hours, remove candy from pan and
turn nougat-side-up onto counter top. Beginning on the 9-
inch side that is covered with nougat, roll jellyroll-style as
tightly as possible and pressing the uncovered caramel to the
back side of the caramel in the roll. Continue rolling candy
back and forth to lengthen the roll. When roll becomes too
long to handle easily, cut in half and roll each half separately.
When rolls are about 1 inch in diameter, cut in 1/2-inch slices.
Pinwheels may be served plain in candy cups or dipped in
tempered chocolate. Stores well in refrigerator if wrapped in
plastic wrap. Makes about 100 pieces.

Tender Marshmallows

Excellent for Easter eggs or for cut marshmallows.

2 (about 1/4-ounce) envelopes unflavored gelatin
1/2 cup cold water
3/4 cup hot water
1 cup light corn syrup, divided
2 cups granulated sugar
1 teaspoon vanilla
About 1/2 cup powdered sugar

Lightly butter a 9-inch square baking pan; set aside. In a small bowl, combine gelatin and cold water. Stir with a spoon until very thick. Allow to stand 5 minutes.

In a 2-quart saucepan, combine hot water, 1/2 cup of the corn syrup and the sugar. Place over high heat and stir with a wooden spoon until mixture comes to a boil. If sugar crystals are present, wash down sides of pan with a wet pastry brush.

Clip on candy thermometer. Cook to 238F (115C) or soft-ball stage. Remove from heat and stir in remaining corn syrup. Pour into medium-size bowl. Using electric mixer at high speed, beat hot syrup, adding gelatin mixture 1 tablespoon at a time. Continue beating until all gelatin is incorporated, candy is thick and has cooled to lukewarm, about 10 minutes. Stir in vanilla. Pour into prepared pan. Cool 3 hours or until marshmallow is firm enough to cut. Using a knife dipped in hot water, cut marshmallows into pieces about 1-3/4-inches square. Roll cut marshmallows in powdered sugar to prevent sticking. Makes about 25 pieces.

Variations

Use different extracts and food colors to vary the flavor.
Roll freshly-cut marshmallows in coconut.

For Marshmallow Easter Eggs—Spoon flour about 1-1/2 inches deep into two 9″ X 13″ baking pans. Using the back of a large spoon or an egg mold, make impressions in the flour, leaving 1/2 inch between holes. When marshmallow is thick and lukewarm, spoon into impressions made in the flour. Pour any excess marshmallow into a buttered pan. Allow to stand several hours until firm. Remove marshmallow eggs from the flour; shake off excess flour. Place flat side down on a waxed paper-lined tray. Dip in tempered dipping chocolate (pages 146-153) or melted compound coating (pages 134, 146-153) and decorate with melted and cooled compound coating (or use royal icing) and purchased royal icing flowers. Makes about 20 2-inch eggs.

Egg molds or a large spoon are used to form impressions in flour-filled baking pan. Lukewarm marshmallow, tinted with food color if desired, is spooned into the impressions.

After several hours, the "set" marshmallow eggs are removed and excess flour is shaken off. The eggs are now ready for dipping in tempered chocolate or compound coating and decorating with icing flowers.

Fruit-Flavored Marshmallows

An electric mixer on a stand is a big help with this recipe as it eliminates constant "hovering" during the prolonged beating. Experiment with different gelatins to vary the taste.

2 (1/4-ounce) envelopes unflavored gelatin
1/4 cup cold water
1 cup boiling water

1/4 cup fruit-flavored gelatin
2 cups granulated sugar
About 1/2 cup powdered sugar

Lightly butter an 9-inch square baking pan; set aside. In a large bowl, combine unflavored gelatin and cold water; let stand 5 minutes. Add boiling water and flavored gelatin; stir with a wooden spoon until dissolved. Add sugar.

Using electric mixer on high speed, beat until mixture is thick and fluffy, about 30 minutes. Pour into prepared pan and let stand at room temperature until firm, about 2 hours. Using a knife dipped in hot water, cut marshmallows into pieces about 1-3/4 inches square. Roll marshmallows in powdered sugar, shaking off excess. Store in an airtight container. Makes 25 pieces.

Variations
After cutting marshmallows, roll in one of the following:
Plain or toasted coconut
A mixture of about 3 tablespoons unsweetened cocoa mixed with about 1 cup powdered sugar
Finely chopped nuts
If the toppings do not stick to the marshmallows, place cut marshmallows one at a time in a strainer and rinse quickly under hot water, then roll in topping. Allow to dry thoroughly before storing in airtight container.

Mazetta

This homemade marshmallow creme is used in many of our recipes.

2 egg whites, at room temperature
3/4 cup light corn syrup

1/4 cup water
1/2 cup sugar

Using electric mixer, beat egg whites in large bowl until stiff; set aside. In a 1-quart saucepan, combine corn syrup, water and sugar. Place over high heat and stir with a wooden spoon until mixture comes to a boil. If sugar crystals are present, wash down sides of the pan with a wet pastry brush.

Clip on candy thermometer. Cook syrup to 242F (120C) or soft-ball stage. Beating constantly with electric mixer, slowly pour hot syrup into egg whites; continue beating several minutes until mixture holds its shape. Use immediately, or refrigerate in a covered container for up to 2 weeks. Makes enough for 3 batches of fondant.

Variation
Thin mazetta with a little hot water for a tasty ice cream topping.

Snicks

These are delicious dipped in chocolate and resemble a famous peanut-caramel-nougat candy bar.

1 recipe Peanut Caramel (page 68)
1 egg white, at room temperature
1 cup light corn syrup
1/2 cup water
1-1/2 cups sugar

3/4 cup creamy peanut butter
1/2 teaspoon vanilla
Tempered dipping chocolate (pages
    146-153), if desired

Prepare Peanut Caramel and pour into a buttered 15″ x 10″ jellyroll pan; set aside. *(This may be made one day ahead, if desired.)*

Using an electric mixer, beat egg white in a medium-size bowl until stiff; set aside. In a 2-quart saucepan, combine corn syrup, water and sugar. Place over high heat and stir constantly with a wooden spoon until mixture comes to a boil. If sugar crystals are present, wash down sides of pan with a wet pastry brush.

Clip on candy thermometer. Cook to 246F (120C) or firm-ball stage. Remove from heat. With electric mixer on high, slowly pour hot syrup over egg white. Beat 2 minutes until well-mixed but still thin. Add peanut butter and vanilla and stir with a wooden spoon until well blended. Pour over caramel, spreading evenly. Chill 3 hours or until firm. Cut into 1-inch squares. Dip in tempered chocolate, if desired. Makes 150 pieces.

Note: This recipe freezes very well.

From upper right: Orange Marmalade Jellies (page 90); Cranberry-Raspberry Jellies (page 91) partially dipped in vanilla coating; Pineapple Jellies with chopped nuts (page 89); Lime Marmalade Jellies (page 90); and Fruit Jam Jellies (page 89).

Jellies & Fruits

These sparkling jewels are colorful, decorative, delicious *and* simple to make. They usually have a base of real fruit or fruit juices and gelatin; sometimes nuts or coconut are added, and they are either rolled in powdered or granulated sugar, or dipped in chocolate or compound coating.

Jellies are not too sweet and they contain little fat so they can be enjoyed by those who are watching their calorie or fat intake. For variety, cut jellies into diamonds, circles, semi-circles, rectangles or sticks in addition to squares. This type of candy should be stored in airtight containers to retain freshness.

Dried fruits were the first sweets enjoyed by man, and they make excellent nutritious treats. The pioneers chopped or ground fruits and nuts and, with the addition of honey, came up with a delightful confection. Included in this chapter is a modernized version of an old recipe for pioneer candy—and we think you will enjoy it.

Cherry cordials, the "mystery candy," is also included in this chapter. Two methods are given—one using firm fondant and the other using melted—and it simply boils down to personal preference. Both work beautifully!

Cordial Fruits

In candymaking, there is nothing as dramatic as the cherry cordial. To the inexperienced candymaker, it seems a great mystery as to how the liquid gets inside the chocolate. Actually, it is quite an easy process, although a bit time-consuming. The liquid part of the cherry chocolate is actually a firm fondant when it is dipped in the chocolate. As the juice from the cherry reacts with the sugar in the fondant, the fondant liquefies and becomes the runny liquid that drips down your chin.

We present two different methods and recipes for making cherry cordials, and suggest you try them both and see which is more successful for you. Both make the best cherry chocolates you will ever eat!

Purchase maraschino cherries that are not too large; by the time you cover them with fondant and chocolate, the cherry becomes much larger than it looks in the bottle. Usually, the larger the bottle, the larger the cherry. If you are going to be making a large number of cherry cordials, you may want to buy them in 2-quart bottles from confectionery suppliers. You can specify the size of cherry you prefer; we like small to medium.

Drain the cherries on paper towels for several hours while you make your fondant. Of course, you could also make the fondant ahead of time and have it on hand. Be sure to reserve the cherry juice in the bottle in case you overestimated the amount of fruit. (Regardless of the method, you will need approximately 100 cherries.)

Cherry cordials must be dipped in chocolate immediately after being covered with fondant. Otherwise, the cordial process will begin on the trays and you will have a wet, gooey mess with which to contend. Have your chocolate ready—and having a helper is very useful.

Cherry Cordials (Method 1)

Use this method when making 100 cherries or less. Also, this is the easier version if you don't have a helper.

About 100 maraschino cherries
1 recipe Cream Fondant (page 24)
2 teaspoons almond extract
1 teaspoon Victorine flavoring or rum extract
Cornstarch (if needed)
Tempered dipping chocolate (pages 146-153)

Thoroughly drain cherries on paper towels. Prepare Cream Fondant, adding flavorings listed above; do not add mazetta.

Cover 2 baking sheets or trays with waxed paper; set aside. If you are right-handed, place a piece of fondant about the size of a large marble in the palm of your left hand. Flatten the fondant with the right hand. Place a well-drained cherry in the center of the fondant in your left hand. Beginning with your right hand, wrap the fondant around the cherry. When it is completely covered with fondant, roll smooth with both hands and place on a waxed paper-lined tray. If fondant is sticky, wash and dry hands thoroughly and dust them with cornstarch. Dip within 1 hour in tempered chocolate. Makes about 100 cherry chocolates.

Method 1: Marble-sized balls of fondant are flattened slightly and wrapped around very well-drained maraschino cherries.

Method 2 (page 88): Cherries, held either by a dipping fork or cherry stem, are coated completely with Melted Cordial Fondant.

Regardless of the dipping method, Cherry Cordials must be covered quickly with tempered dipping chocolate. Follow procedure described on pages 148-152.

Cherry Cordials (Method 2)

This method is faster if you are doing a large quantity of cherries, or if a second person helps. One can dip cherries in the fondant, the other in the chocolate.

About 125 maraschino cherries　　　　**Maraschino cherry juice (if needed)**
1 recipe Melted Cordial Fondant (page 42)　　**Tempered dipping chocolate (pages 146-153)**

Thoroughly drain cherries on paper towels. Prepare Melted Cordial Fondant. Cover 2 baking sheets or trays with waxed paper; set aside.

Place half the set-up fondant in the top of a double boiler. Place over medium heat and stir gently with a wooden spoon as fondant melts. Clip on candy thermometer. Stirring gently, melt fondant to about 150F (65C). When fondant has completely melted, use a dipping fork, fondue fork or table fork and drop cherries 1 at a time into fondant; dunk the cherry under the fondant to coat completely. Using fork, remove cherry and place on waxed paper-lined baking sheet.

If fondant appears too thick, thin with 1 tablespoon maraschino cherry juice; this also adds a pretty color to the fondant. Continue dunking each cherry until about 1/2 of the melted fondant is used. Add remaining fondant and heat to 150F (65C). Continue with remaining cherries.

Cherries need to cool for several minutes until the heat from the fondant has left before being dipped in tempered chocolate. Makes about 125 cherry chocolates.

Variations
Cherry Cordials with Stems—Use Method 2 and maraschino cherries with stems. Hold cherries by stems and dip each individually in the melted fondant. When cool, dip in tempered dipping chocolate (pages 146-153), again holding by the stem. Place on waxed paper.

Cherry Cordials with a Kick—Drain cherries on paper towels overnight (they will appear shriveled). Place drained cherries in empty cherry jar and cover with your favorite rum or brandy. Replace lid and store at room temperature for 2 to 3 weeks. Taste occasionally; when desired flavor has been obtained, drain and proceed with either Cherry Cordials (Method 1) or Cherry Cordials (Method 2).

Pineapple Cordials—Pineapple cordials can be made using either of the two methods described for cherry cordials. They are absolutely wonderful, but they do take a lot of work. Mainly, be aware that pineapple is more difficult to handle as it is much stickier than cherries.

Select either canned pineapple tidbits or slices; fresh or frozen won't work. If you use sliced pineapple, cut it into wedges about 1/2 inch wide. You must drain the pineapple very well, and work fast when covering with fondant. As you might imagine, pineapple does not make a smooth, round piece of candy but, instead, a rather irregular, oblong-shaped piece.

Fruit Jam Jellies

Use your favorite fruit jam. We are especially fond of red raspberry.

1 cup jam
1/2 cup water
3/4 cup sugar
2 (1/4-ounce) envelopes unflavored gelatin

1/4 teaspoon citric acid
Cornstarch or powdered sugar
About 1/2 cup powdered sugar
A few drops red food color

Butter a 9" x 5" loaf pan; set aside. In a 2-quart saucepan, combine jam, water, sugar, gelatin and citric acid. Place over medium heat and stir constantly with a wooden spoon until mixture comes to a boil. Boil 2 minutes, stirring constantly to prevent scorching. Pour into prepared pan. Refrigerate 3 hours or until firm.

Lightly dust waxed paper with cornstarch or powdered sugar. Using a spatula, loosen candy from pan and flip onto waxed paper. Cut into 1-inch squares and roll in powdered sugar. Store in an airtight container. Makes 64 pieces.

Variations
Add 1/2 cup chopped nuts before pouring into cooling pan.
Rather than rolling in powdered sugar, dip in tempered dipping chocolate (pages 146-153) or in melted compound coating (pages 134, 146-153).

Pineapple Jellies

A refreshing, no-fat treat.

1 (20-ounce) can crushed pineapple, undrained
2 (1/4-ounce) envelopes plain gelatin
1-1/2 cups sugar

1 tablespoon lemon juice
Cornstarch or powdered sugar
Powdered sugar or tempered dipping chocolate (pages 146-153)

Butter an 8-inch square baking pan; set aside. In a small bowl, combine 1/2 cup of the pineapple and the gelatin; stir until well mixed. Set aside. In a 2-quart saucepan, combine 3/4 cup of the pineapple with sugar and lemon juice. Stir with a wooden spoon until well-mixed. (You will have extra pineapple.)

Place over medium heat and stir constantly until mixture comes to a boil. Boil 10 minutes, stirring constantly to prevent scorching. Add gelatin-pineapple mixture and boil, stirring constantly, 5 minutes more. Pour into prepared pan and refrigerate overnight. Lightly dust waxed paper with cornstarch or powdered sugar. Using a spatula, loosen candy from pan and flip onto waxed paper. Cut into 1-inch squares; roll in powdered sugar or dip in tempered chocolate. Store in an airtight container. Makes 64 pieces.

Variation
Add 1 cup chopped nuts or coconut before pouring candy into cooling pan.

Orange Marmalade Jellies

A colorful summer candy.

1 cup orange marmalade, whipped lightly
  in blender
1/2 cup water
3/4 cup sugar

1 (3-ounce) package orange-flavored gelatin
2 (1/4-ounce) envelopes unflavored gelatin
Cornstarch or powdered sugar
About 1/2 cup powdered sugar

Butter a 9″ x 5″ loaf pan; set aside. In a heavy 2-quart saucepan, combine marmalade, sugar and gelatins. Place over medium heat and stir constantly with a wooden spoon until mixture comes to a boil. Boil 2 minutes, stirring constantly to prevent scorching. Pour into prepared pan. Refrigerate 2 hours or until firm.

Lightly dust waxed paper with cornstarch or powdered sugar. Using a spatula, loosen candy from pan and flip onto waxed paper. Cut into 1-inch squares and roll in powdered sugar. Store in an airtight container. Makes 64 pieces.

Variations
Instead of rolling jellies in powdered sugar, dip in tempered dipping chocolate (pages 146-153) or in melted compound coating (pages 134, 146-153).
For Lemon-Lime or Lime Marmalade Jellies—Use lemon or lime marmalade and lime-flavored gelatin in place of orange marmalade and orange-flavored gelatin.

Orange Sticks

The tang of citrus with the coolness of a jelly.

3 (1/4-ounce) envelopes unflavored gelatin
1/2 cup cold water
2 cups sugar
1/2 cup hot water
4 teaspoons grated fresh orange peel
2 teaspoons grated fresh lemon peel

2 tablespoons fresh orange juice
2 tablespoons fresh lemon juice
1/4 teaspoon orange food color
Cornstarch
Tempered dipping chocolate (pages
  146-153), if desired

Butter an 8-inch square baking pan; set aside. In a small bowl, sprinkle gelatin over cold water and let stand about 5 minutes to soften. In a 2-quart saucepan, combine sugar and hot water. Place over high heat and stir constantly until mixture comes to a boil. Add softened gelatin; reduce heat and simmer, stirring constantly, 5 minutes. Stir in orange and lemon peels, juices and food color. Refrigerate 20 minutes. Pour through a strainer into prepared pan. Refrigerate until firm, several hours or overnight.

Lightly dust waxed paper with cornstarch. Using a spatula, loosen candy from pan and flip onto waxed paper. Cut into long sticks 1/4″ x 2″. Roll in additional cornstarch to prevent pieces from sticking. Serve plain, or shake off excess cornstarch and dip in tempered chocolate. Makes 128 pieces.

Cranberry-Raspberry Jellies

This vibrantly-colored candy is just right for the holidays or, dipped in compound coating, these jellies make a refreshing summer treat.

1 (16-ounce) can jellied cranberry sauce
1/2 cup water
2 (1/4-ounce) envelopes unflavored gelatin
1 (3-ounce) package raspberry-flavored
   gelatin

3/4 cup sugar
Cornstarch or powdered sugar
Melted compound coating (pages 134,
   146-153), if desired

Butter a 9″ x 5″ loaf pan or 9-inch square baking pan; set aside. In a 2-quart saucepan, combine cranberry sauce, water, gelatins and sugar. Place over low heat and stir constantly with a wooden spoon until mixture comes to a boil. Boil 5 minutes, stirring constantly to prevent scorching. Pour into prepared pan. Refrigerate 4 hours or until firm.

   Lightly dust waxed paper with cornstarch or powdered sugar. Using a spatula, loosen candy from pan and flip onto waxed paper. Cut into 1-inch squares. Serve chilled, either plain or dipped in compound coating. Makes 81 pieces.

Pauline's Applettes

Especially popular during the Christmas holidays, but enjoyable year-round. This recipe gives a very tender candy; if you prefer a chewier consistency, add 1 tablespoon cornstarch to the gelatin mixture.

2 (1/4-ounce) envelopes unflavored gelatin
1-1/4 cups applesauce
1 tablespoon lemon juice
1-1/2 cups sugar
1 cup chopped nuts or flaked coconut

1/2 teaspoon vanilla
Cornstarch or powdered sugar
Powdered sugar, tempered dipping
   chocolate (pages 146-153) or melted
   compound coating (pages 146-153)

Butter an 8-inch square baking dish; set aside. In a small bowl, sprinkle gelatin over 1/2 cup of the applesauce; stir until well-mixed. Set aside. In a 1-quart saucepan, combine remaining apple-sauce, lemon juice and sugar and stir well. Place over medium heat and stir constantly until mixture comes to a boil. Boil 10 minutes, stirring constantly. Add gelatin-applesauce mixture and boil, stirring constantly, 5 minutes more. Remove from heat and add nuts or coconut and vanilla. Pour into prepared pan. Refrigerate 24 hours.

   Lightly dust waxed paper with cornstarch or powdered sugar. Using a spatula, loosen candy from pan and flip onto waxed paper. Cut into 1-inch squares. Roll in powdered sugar, or dip in tempered chocolate or compound coating. Store in an airtight container. Makes 64 pieces.

Apricot Balls

So good—and so good for you.

2 pounds dried apricots
1-1/2 pounds shredded coconut

1 (14-ounce) can sweetened condensed milk
About 1/2 cup powdered sugar

Using food processor or food grinder, coarsely grind apricots and coconut together. Place in a medium-size bowl. Add condensed milk and stir with a wooden spoon until combined. Place in refrigerator overnight. Form into 1-inch balls and roll in powdered sugar. Store in an airtight container in refrigerator up to 3 weeks. Makes about 100 pieces.

Dried Fruit Candy

Vary the ingredients and amounts to suit your taste.

1 cup pitted dates, chopped
1/2 cup pitted prunes
1/2 cup raisins
1/2 cup drained crushed pineapple
1/3 cup dried apricots

Slivered peel from 1/2 orange
1-1/2 cups fruit juice or water
1-1/2 cups chopped pecans
About 3 cups flaked or macaroon coconut

In a 2-quart saucepan, combine dates, prunes, raisins, pineapple, apricots, peel and juice. Place over medium heat and stir with a wooden spoon until mixture comes to a boil. Reduce heat to low and remove spoon; cover and simmer 30 minutes or until all liquid is absorbed. Mixture should resemble thick jam; if it is too thin, continue cooking, stirring constantly, until mixture thickens. Remove from heat and mash fruit with a vegetable masher. Stir in pecans. Refrigerate 1 hour.

Place coconut in medium-size bowl. Using a teaspoon, form fruit mixture into 1-inch balls. Add to coconut and roll until thoroughly covered. Refrigerate until served. Store in an airtight container in refrigerator up to 3 weeks. Makes 50 balls.

Pioneer Fruit Candy

The early settlers used a variety of fruits to make their treats.

1 pound raisins
1/2 pound dried figs
1/2 pound pitted dates
1 cup pitted prunes

Peel from 1 orange
1 cup chopped nuts
1/4 cup orange juice
About 1 cup powdered sugar

Using food processor or food grinder, finely grind raisins, figs, dates, prunes and peel. In a medium-size bowl, combine fruits and nuts. Add juice and mix well with a wooden spoon. Form into 1-inch balls and roll in powdered sugar. Place in an airtight container and refrigerate 24 hours to blend flavors. Store in the refrigerator up to 4 weeks. Makes 50 balls.

Fruit Twinkles

These slightly chewy little jewels can also be rolled in finely chopped nuts or in graham cracker crumbs instead of coconut. The results are a bit more cookie- than candy-like—but they taste delicious either way. Feel free to vary the fruits and the proportions to suit your fancy. (Pauline is partial to a combination of 3/4 cup dates and 1/4 cup apricots.)

1/4 cup evaporated milk
1/2 cup miniature marshmallows
1 cup finely cut, firmly packed, soft dried
 fruit (dates, pears, apricots, peaches or
 apples or a combination)
1/4 cup chopped or diced maraschino
 cherries

1-1/2 cups graham cracker crumbs
1/2 cup chopped walnuts, pecans or
 almonds, if desired
1/2 teaspoon almond extract
About 1-1/2 cups flake coconut or about 1
 cup macaroon coconut

Combine milk and marshmallows in a 1-quart saucepan. Place over medium heat and stir constantly until marshmallows are melted. Remove from heat. Add dried fruit, cherries, graham cracker crumbs, nuts and almond extract and mix well. Let stand until cool.

Pour coconut into shallow dish or plate. Add fruit mixture by teaspoonfuls and roll until well covered with coconut. Form into oblong or ball shapes. Store in airtight container in refrigerator. Makes 20 to 25 candies.

Variations
Use 1/4 teaspoon cinnamon in place of almond extract.
Use orange extract in place of almond extract.

From upper left: Pauline's Peanut Brittle (page 97); Amy's Toffee (page 105); Coconut-Cashew Brittle (page 98); Glazed Almonds (page 100); and Ruth's Pecan Brittle (page 96).

Brittles & Hard Candies

Who can forget the wonderful aroma of peanut brittle as it cooks—or the experience of an all-day sucker that really lasts all day. This chapter delves into the delicious subject of hard candies and brittles, which also includes toffees, taffys, lollipops and mints. This candy category is closely related in two primary respects: first, these candies are all cooked to a high temperature and, second, they become sticky if not stored in airtight containers as soon as they are completely cooled.

Toffee is a wonderfully crisp candy that melts in your mouth. It should be tender—not chewy—and when covered with chocolate and nuts, it becomes even tastier. Toffee requires a lot of attention while cooking to avoid separation of the butter and sugar. After cooling, this candy should be stored in airtight containers and allowed to age; it becomes more tender after several days—but can be kept for several weeks in this manner.

Hard candies are easy to prepare and, with proper flavoring and color, become a real favorite of both children and adults. Whether you pour the batch in a sheet and break it up, or mold it separately as for lollipops, it looks pretty and tastes great.

Nut brittles are fast becoming a favorite in our family. The aroma of the nuts roasting in the hot syrup is memorable. Peanut brittle is a long-time favorite. Even the older generation can enjoy our recipe because it is stretched thin and doesn't stick to teeth. Pecan brittle is a new recipe we developed just for this book. It's guaranteed to be "more-ish."

Try your hand at pulled buttermints—small creamy pillows that melt in your mouth. They are a little tricky, but well worth the effort.

As hard candies absorb moisture from the air, causing the candy to become sticky, they will not be as successful on humid days as they are on drier days. Layer these candies with waxed paper to prevent pieces from sticking together—and never store in the refrigerator as this makes them even stickier.

Ruth's Pecan Brittle

Ruth's original recipe—and it is irresistible!

4 cups pecan pieces	1/2 cup butter
1/4 cup whipping cream	1/2 teaspoon salt
1/4 cup light corn syrup	1/2 teaspoon baking soda
1/4 cup water	1/2 teaspoon vanilla
1 cup sugar	

Butter a 15" x 10" jellyroll pan; set aside. Preheat oven to 200F (95C). Place pecans in a 9" x 13" baking pan. Keep warm in oven while candy is cooking.

In a heavy 2-quart saucepan, combine cream, corn syrup, water and sugar. Place over medium-high heat and stir with a wooden spoon until mixture comes to a boil. If sugar crystals are present, wash down sides of pan with a wet pastry brush.

Clip on candy thermometer. Cook syrup to 295F (150C). Stir in butter, which will reduce temperature. Continue cooking syrup to 280F (140C) or soft-crack stage. Remove from heat; stir in salt, baking soda and vanilla. Add warm pecans and stir until nuts are well-coated. Pour onto baking sheet.

Using 2 forks and working quickly, separate brittle into fairly large pieces. Allow to cool completely. Store in airtight containers. This candy improves with a few days aging. Makes about 30 pieces.

Pauline's Peanut Brittle

An old-time favorite stretched thin so even the old-timers can enjoy it.

1/2 cup light corn syrup
1/2 cup water
1 cup sugar
1 cup raw Spanish peanuts
2 tablespoons butter
1/2 teaspoon salt
1 teaspoon vanilla
1 teaspoon baking soda

Butter a 15″ X 10″ jellyroll pan or 15-inch pizza pan; set aside. In a heavy 3-quart saucepan, combine corn syrup, water and sugar. Place over high heat and stir with a wooden spoon until mixture comes to a boil. When syrup starts to thicken, stir in peanuts. Stirring constantly, cook until the peanuts smell cooked and the syrup bubbles are a pale straw color.

Remove from heat and stir in butter, salt and vanilla. *Use caution as this will cause steam and could burn your hand.* Stir in baking soda until it foams. Pour onto baking sheet and allow to cool for several minutes.

Using 2 forks, or buttered finger tips, begin stretching the edges away from the mass of brittle. Work your way around the pan, pulling off pieces as you stretch. Place these pieces on the counter top or on another baking sheet; turn the pieces upside down as this will cause the peanuts to stay in the center of the candy, rather than sink to the bottom. Continue in this manner until all the brittle has been stretched. Allow to cool completely. Store in airtight containers. Makes 1 pound.

STRETCHING PEANUT BRITTLE

Cooked brittle is poured onto a pizza pan or baking sheet and cooled briefly.

Using buttered finger tips or forks, the edges of the brittle are stretched away from the center, pulling the brittle very thin. The thinness, as well as the recipe proportions, is what makes this brittle easy to eat and why it doesn't stick to the teeth.

Coconut-Cashew Brittle

Ribbon coconut, which is about 1/2 inch wide, works best for this recipe. It is available at many nut shops and health food stores, or through the sources on our supplier list on page 155.

1 cup light corn syrup	3 cups cashews
1 cup water	3 cups ribbon coconut
2-1/2 cups sugar	1/2 teaspoon salt

Set aside a 15″ x 10″ jellyroll pan. In a heavy 4-quart saucepan, combine corn syrup, water and sugar. Place over high heat and stir occasionally with a wooden spoon until mixture comes to a boil. If sugar crystals are present, wash down sides of pan with a wet pastry brush.

Clip on candy thermometer. Cook syrup to 232F (115C) or soft-ball stage. Add nuts and stir constantly until syrup turns a light-brown color and temperature reaches 287F (140C) or soft-crack stage. Remove from heat and stir in coconut and salt. Mix until coconut is well-coated with syrup and mixture is golden-brown. Pour onto baking sheet and allow brittle to cool several minutes.

Using 2 forks and working quickly, separate brittle into fairly large pieces. Allow to cool completely. Store in airtight containers. This candy improves with a few days aging. Makes about 2 pounds.

Butter Crunch

An economical toffee made with both butter and margarine.

1 cup chopped pecans or walnuts	3 tablespoons water
1/2 cup butter	1 cup sugar
1/2 cup margarine	1/2 cup sweet or milk chocolate, if desired

Line an 8-inch square baking pan with foil; cover bottom with nuts and set aside. In a heavy 2-quart saucepan, combine butter, margarine, water and sugar. Place over high heat and stir constantly with a wooden spoon—mixture will foam. Cook, stirring constantly, until mixture becomes a light tan color; *do not let it get brown.* Remove from heat and pour over nuts. Using back of wooden spoon, spread mixture evenly over nuts. Cool at room temperature 1 hour.

Melt chocolate; spread over top of candy. Let stand at room temperature for 24 hours. Break into irregular-sized pieces. Store in an airtight container. Makes 35 pieces.

Pecan Crunch

A delicious combination of pecans and butter.

1 cup pecan pieces
1/2 teaspoon baking soda
1/2 cup butter
1/4 cup water

1-1/2 teaspoons cider vinegar
1 cup sugar
1/4 teaspoon salt

Butter a 15" x 10" jellyroll pan; set aside. In a small bowl, combine pecans and baking soda; set aside. In a heavy 4-quart saucepan, combine butter, water, vinegar, sugar and salt. Place over high heat and stir occasionally with a wooden spoon until mixture comes to a boil. If sugar crystals are present, wash down sides of pan with a wet pastry brush.

Clip on candy thermometer. Cook, stirring occasionally, to 290F (145C) or soft-crack stage. Stir in pecan-soda mixture until well-blended. Pour into prepared pan. Cool 2 hours. To serve, break into pieces. Store in an airtight container. Makes about 35 pieces.

Cashew Crunch

A cross between toffee and brittle.

1 cup butter
2 tablespoons water
2 tablespoons light corn syrup

1 cup sugar
1 cup salted cashews
1 teaspoon vanilla

Butter a 15" x 10" jellyroll pan; set aside. In a heavy 2-quart saucepan, melt butter. Add water. With a wooden spoon, stir in corn syrup and sugar. Place over high heat and stir constantly with a wooden spoon until mixture comes to a boil. If sugar crystals are present, wash down sides of pan with wet pastry brush.

Clip on candy thermometer. Cook syrup to 300F (150C) or hard-crack stage. Remove from heat and stir in nuts and vanilla. Pour into prepared pan and spread thin. When completely cool, break into pieces. Store in an airtight container. Makes about 1-1/2 pounds.

Walnut Crunch

Walnuts and butter team up to make a spectacular brittle.

1/2 cup butter	1 cup firmly packed brown sugar
1/4 cup water	3/4 cup finely chopped walnuts
1 tablespoon honey	

Line an 8-inch square baking pan with foil; set aside. In a heavy 1-quart saucepan, combine butter, water, honey and brown sugar. Place over high heat and stir with a wooden spoon until mixture comes to a boil. If sugar crystals are present, wash down sides of the pan with a wet pastry brush.

Clip on candy thermometer. Cook syrup to 280F (145C) or soft-crack stage. Stir in walnuts. Pour into prepared pan. Cool at room temperature. Break into pieces and store in an airtight container. Makes 3/4 pound.

Glazed Almonds

A surprisingly easy recipe.

1/2 cup water	2 cups whole raw almonds
1 cup sugar	

Set aside an ungreased baking sheet. In a heavy 2-quart skillet, combine water and sugar. Place over high heat and stir with a wooden spoon until mixture comes to a boil. Add almonds and stir continuously. Reduce heat to medium and stir almonds until mixture foams and turns to sugar. Continue stirring as almonds become coated with sugar; sugar will begin to remelt and caramelize on the almonds. Remove from heat and turn out onto baking sheet. Using 2 forks, separate almonds into single nuts. Cool. Makes about 250 glazed nuts.

Variations
For Glazed Orange Almonds—Add 2 tablespoons grated orange peel at the beginning of cooking.
For Glazed Spiced Almonds—Add 1/4 teaspoon cinnamon at the beginning of cooking.
For Glazed Rose Almonds—At the end of cooking, sprinkle nuts with 2 teaspoons rose water (available at many pharmacies) and stir well.

Candied Pecans

My friend Gayla's favorite recipe.

2 cups coarsely chopped pecans
2 cups sugar

Butter a baking sheet; set aside. Preheat oven to 300F (150C). Spread pecans in an 8-inch square baking pan. Place in oven to crisp for 8 minutes, stirring every 2 minutes. While nuts are crisping, place sugar in a medium-size skillet over medium-high heat. With a wooden spoon, stir sugar until it melts and turns into a golden syrup. *Use caution as this syrup is extremely hot and could damage the skin.* Remove nuts from oven and add to hot syrup, stirring until nuts are well-coated. Pour out onto prepared pan to cool. When completely cooled, break into pieces. Store in an airtight container. Makes about 1-1/2 pounds.

Sugared Walnuts

For variety, try this recipe using pecans.

2-1/2 cups walnut halves
1/2 cup water
1 cup sugar

1 teaspoon cinnamon
1/2 teaspoon salt
1-1/2 teaspoons vanilla

Preheat oven to 375F (190C). Spread walnuts on a 15″ x 10″ jellyroll pan. Place in oven for 5 minutes. Turn oven off, leaving nuts in warm oven. Line a baking sheet with waxed paper and set aside.

In a heavy 2-quart saucepan, combine water, sugar, cinnamon and salt. Place over high heat and stir with a wooden spoon until mixture comes to a boil. If sugar crystals are present, wash down sides of pan with a wet pastry brush.

Clip on candy thermometer. Cook syrup to 238F (115C) or soft-ball stage. Remove from heat; remove thermometer. With a wooden spoon, beat 1 minute or until mixture is creamy. Add vanilla and warm nuts and stir until well-coated. Spread on waxed paper to cool. Using 2 forks, separate walnuts into single nuts. Store in an airtight container. Makes 1-1/2 pounds.

Lollipops

These all-day suckers really last all day. If you'd like to add small candies or other decorations, arrange them on the lollipops as the syrup is cooling in the molds or on the baking sheet.

1 cup light corn syrup	Flavoring and food color (suggestions
1 cup water	follow)
2 cups sugar	10 sucker sticks

Prepare sucker molds or butter a baking sheet; set aside. In a 2-quart saucepan, combine corn syrup, water and sugar. Place over high heat and stir with a wooden spoon until mixture comes to a boil. If sugar crystals are present, wash down sides of pan with a wet pastry brush.

Clip on candy thermometer. Cook syrup to 300F (150C) or hard-crack stage. Remove from heat. Add flavoring and food color and stir with a wooden spoon until blended. Pour into molds, adding sucker sticks, or pour free-form or in 2-inch circles on baking sheet and place a sucker stick in each lollipop. Cool at room temperature. Makes about 10 lollipops.

Flavor suggestions:
For Root Beer—Add 1 teaspoon root beer concentrate, which is available in supermarkets; no additional flavoring or food color is needed.
For Cinnamon—Add 1/8 teaspoon oil of cinnamon and red food color.
For Green Apple—Add 1/4 teaspoon green apple flavoring, a pinch or drop of citric acid and green food color.
For Bubble Gum—Add 1/4 teaspoon bubble gum flavoring and pink food color.
For Grape—Add 1/4 teaspoon grape flavoring, a pinch or drop of citric acid and purple food color.
For Cherry—Add 1/4 teaspoon cherry flavoring, a pinch or drop of citric acid and red food color.
For Orange—Add 1/4 teaspoon oil of orange, a pinch or drop of citric acid and orange food color.
For Lemon—Add 1/4 teaspoon oil of lemon, a pinch or drop of citric acid and yellow food color.
For Lime—Add 1/4 teaspoon oil of lime, a pinch or drop of citric acid and green food color.
For Licorice—Add 1/4 teaspoon oil of anise and black paste food color.

Note: White-white liquid icing color makes the lollipops opaque. Check supplier list on page 155 for sources of the more unusual flavorings and food colors.

Assorted molded and free-form Lollipops

Lacy Roll-Ups & Bows

Tie a bow or ribbon around each piece for a special occasion.

1/2 cup butter
1 cup all-purpose flour
1/2 cup light corn syrup

2/3 cup firmly packed brown sugar
1 cup chopped pecans

Butter a 15" x 10" jellyroll pan; set aside. In a heavy 2-quart saucepan, melt butter. Using a wooden spoon, stir in flour. Add corn syrup, brown sugar and pecans. Place over high heat and bring to a boil. Reduce heat to medium and boil, stirring constantly, 7 minutes. Pour into prepared pan. Let stand until cool enough to handle, about 1 minute. Cut candy into 2-inch squares. While still warm, pinch square into bow shape, or roll up into a cylindrical shape. Allow to cool completely. Store in an airtight container. Makes about 20 pieces.

Almond Toffee

Dipped in chocolate, rolled in almonds and wrapped in squares of gold foil, this recipe is reminiscent of a very popular commercial candy.

1/2 cup light corn syrup
1/4 cup water
1-1/2 cups sugar

1 cup blanched almonds, sliced or chopped
1 cup butter

Butter a 15" x 10" jellyroll pan; set aside. In an electric frying pan, combine corn syrup, water and sugar. Set temperature to 360F (180C). Stirring constantly with a wooden spoon, bring mixture to a boil. Add almonds and butter; stir until almonds are brown. Pour candy into prepared pan. As candy begins to set, score lines with a heavy knife. Allow candy to cool completely at room temperature. Break candy along scored lines. Store in an airtight container. Makes 1-1/2 pounds (about 35 pieces).

Variation
Dip each piece in tempered dipping chocolate (pages 146-153) and roll in chopped almonds.

Amy's Toffee

Cousin Amy's terrific toffee!

4 cups pecans, finely chopped
2 cups (1 pound) butter
1/2 cup water
1/4 cup light corn syrup
2-1/2 cups sugar
1 pound milk chocolate
4 cups walnuts, finely chopped

Butter a 12″ x 18″ baking sheet; cover with pecans and set aside. In a heavy 3-quart saucepan, combine butter, water, corn syrup and sugar. Place over high heat and stir with a wooden spoon until mixture comes to a boil. Continue stirring until mixture begins to thicken. Reduce heat to low; remove wooden spoon.

Clip on candy thermometer. Cook syrup to 290F (145C) or soft-crack stage. Remove from heat and pour over pecans. Cool at room temperature 1 hour.

Melt chocolate; spread over top of toffee. Sprinkle warm chocolate with walnuts, then press lightly so nuts adhere. Allow to stand at room temperature 24 hours. Break into irregular pieces. Store in an airtight container. Makes 4 to 5 pounds (about 150 pieces).

MAKING TOFFEE

Toffee sometimes separates during cooking, leaving a buttery looking layer on the surface and a thicker mixture underneath.

To correct the separation, add about 1/2 cup of hot water and stir well. You may need to add additional hot water, but this trick will save the batch of toffee.

Syrup is poured—without scraping the saucepan—onto a chilled, well-buttered jellyroll pan or marble slab.

As the edges begin to cool, fold them into the center of the warm candy. This keeps the edges soft and helps the taffy cool evenly, which makes pulling easier.

Delbert's Butter Toffee

A fellow candymaker shares his special recipe for fantastic toffee. Be sure to use AA grade sweet cream (salted) butter. A candy thermometer is difficult, at best, to attach to an electric frying pan, but it does give the best indication of when the candy is done. When you think it's getting close, you can check by holding the thermometer in the syrup and carefully tilting the pan.

1 pound AA grade sweet cream butter
2/3 cup water
2 cups sugar
1 cup chopped almonds

Butter a 12'' x 18'' baking sheet; set aside. In an electric frying pan, combine butter and water. Set temperature on highest setting. Add sugar and stir constantly with a wooden spoon until mixture comes to a boil. Wash down sides of pan with a wet pastry brush to dissolve sugar crystals. Add almonds and stir until they turn golden-brown—about 290F (145C) if using a candy thermometer. Pour into prepared pan and let candy stand at room temperature to cool completely. Break into irregular pieces. Store in an airtight container. Makes about 2 pounds.

Variation
Spread top of unbroken candy with melted chocolate and sprinkle with chopped nuts. When chocolate has set, turn candy over and repeat so both sides are covered with chocolate and nuts.

Pulled Taffy

The real old-fashioned type. Glycerine, available at many pharmacies, is what gives this taffy its slightly soft-yet chewy texture.

1 tablespoon butter
1-3/4 cups water
1 cup light corn syrup
2 cups sugar
1/2 teaspoon salt
1/2 teaspoon glycerine
2 tablespoons butter
1 teaspoon vanilla

Butter a 15″ x 10″ jellyroll pan or marble slab with 1 tablespoon butter; chill jellyroll pan in refrigerator.

In a heavy 4-quart saucepan, combine water, corn syrup, sugar, salt and glycerine. Place over high heat and stir constantly with a wooden spoon until mixture comes to a boil. If sugar crystals are present, wash down sides of pan with a wet pastry brush.

Clip on candy thermometer. Cook syrup to 265F (130C) or hard-ball stage. Remove from heat and let stand for 3 minutes. Stir in remaining 2 tablespoons butter and the vanilla. Remove from heat and, without scraping, pour into chilled pan or onto marble. Let stand until lukewarm, 5 to 10 minutes; as taffy cools, fold edges into the center of the warm candy (this softens the edges while the center cools).

When candy is cool enough to handle, butter fingers liberally and begin pulling taffy. Pull and stretch taffy until it begins to lighten in color, becomes more elastic and springs back. Parallel ridges will also form on the surface.

When taffy is ready for cutting, pull into a rope about 3/4 inch in diameter. Using scissors or a heavy knife, cut taffy in pieces about 1 inch long. Wrap in squares of waxed paper or plastic wrap. Makes about 1 pound or 50 pieces.

Variations
For Mint Taffy—Add 4 drops oil of peppermint in place of the vanilla.
For Chocolate Taffy—Add 2 tablespoons unsweetened cocoa just before pulling.
For Orange Taffy—Add 1 teaspoon orange extract and a few drops of orange food color in place of the vanilla.
For Nut Taffy—Add 3/4 cup finely chopped nuts along with the vanilla.

When the taffy is cool enough to handle, pull it with buttered hands until it lightens in color, becomes more elastic and develops parallel ridges. (Unless you have a lot of arm muscles, you will find it easier to share the pulling with a friend or 2.)

When the taffy is pulled, stretch it into a rope about 3/4 inch thick. Using scissors or a heavy knife, cut the candy quickly into pieces about 1 inch long and wrap it in squares of waxed paper or plastic wrap.

Anne's Honey Taffy

Vary this old-fashioned recipe by using different kinds of honey.

1/2 cup water	1 cup sugar
1/3 cup honey	

Butter a 15″ x 10″ jellyroll pan or a marble slab; chill jellyroll pan in refrigerator while candy is cooking.

In a heavy 2-quart saucepan, combine water, honey and sugar. Place over medium heat and stir with a wooden spoon until mixture comes to a boil. If sugar crystals are present, wash down sides of pan with a wet pastry brush.

Clip on candy thermometer. Cook syrup to 290F (145C) or soft-crack stage. Remove from heat and, without scraping, pour into chilled jellyroll pan or onto marble. Let stand until lukewarm, 5 to 10 minutes; as taffy cools, fold edges into the center of the warm candy (this softens the edges while the center cools).

When candy is cool enough to handle, butter fingers liberally and begin pulling taffy. Pull and stretch taffy until it becomes very light in color, more elastic and springs back. Parallel ridges will also form on the surface.

When taffy is ready for cutting, pull into a rope about 1/2 inch in diameter. Using scissors or a heavy knife, cut taffy in pieces about 1 inch long. Wrap in squares of waxed paper or plastic wrap. Makes about 1/2 pound or 25 pieces.

Cream & Honey Taffy

If you want a stronger-flavored candy, choose a dark, strong-flavored honey. The addition of cream tends to make this candy a little softer.

2 cups light, mild honey	1 cup sugar
1 cup whipping cream	

Butter a 9″ x 13″ baking sheet or a marble slab; chill jellyroll pan in refrigerator while candy is cooking.

In a heavy 4-quart saucepan, combine honey, cream and sugar. Place over medium heat and stir with a wooden spoon until mixture comes to a boil. If sugar crystals are present, wash down sides of pan with a wet pastry brush.

Clip on candy thermometer. Cook syrup to 290F (145C) or soft-crack stage. Remove from heat and, without scraping, pour into chilled baking sheet or onto marble. Let stand until lukewarm, 5 to 10 minutes; as candy cools, fold edges into the center of the warm candy (this softens the edges while the center cools).

When candy is cool enough to handle, butter fingers and begin pulling taffy. Pull and stretch taffy until parallel ridges form and candy begins to lose its gloss. Pull into a rope approximately 1/2 inch in diameter. Using buttered scissors, cut taffy in pieces about 1 inch long. Wrap in squares of waxed paper or plastic wrap. Makes about 50 pieces.

Grandma's Molasses Taffy

Molasses gives this taffy a golden color.

1 tablespoon butter	2 cups sugar
2/3 cup water	1 cup light molasses
1/3 cup light corn syrup	2 tablespoons butter

Butter a 9" x 13" baking sheet or a marble slab; chill baking sheet in refrigerator while candy is cooking.

In a 2-quart saucepan, combine water, corn syrup and sugar. Place over high heat and stir with a wooden spoon until mixture comes to a boil. If sugar crystals are present, wash down sides of pan with a wet pastry brush.

Clip on candy thermometer. Cook syrup to 245F (120C) or firm-ball stage. Stir in molasses and butter. Stirring occasionally, cook to 260F (125C) or hard-ball stage. Remove from heat and, without scraping, pour into chilled baking sheet or onto marble. Let stand until lukewarm, 5 to 10 minutes; as taffy cools, fold edges into the center of the warm candy (this softens the edges while the center cools).

When candy is cool enough to handle, butter fingers liberally and begin pulling taffy. Pull and stretch taffy until it becomes very light in color, more elastic and springs back. Parallel ridges will also form on the surface.

When taffy is ready for cutting, pull into a rope about 1/2 inch in diameter. Using scissors or a heavy knife, cut taffy in pieces about 1 inch long. Wrap in squares of waxed paper or plastic wrap. Makes about 1 pound or 50 pieces.

Ruth's Buttermints

These lovely little mint pillows just melt in your mouth. This is probably the trickiest recipe in the book and we advise that you read the "tips" before starting.

1 cup water
1/2 cup butter
3 cups sugar

1-1/2 teaspoons peppermint extract or 6 drops oil of peppermint
About 5 drops food color, if desired

Butter a marble slab or a 15″ x 10″ jellyroll pan; chill jellyroll pan in refrigerator while candy is cooking.

In a heavy 4-quart saucepan with a lid, combine water and butter. Cook over high heat until butter is melted. Using a wooden spoon, stir in sugar. Remove spoon and bring mixture to a boil. Reduce heat to medium-high and cover pan for 3 minutes; this will wash down sugar crystals from the pan. *This recipe will grain very easily if any sugar crystals are present.*

Clip on candy thermometer. Cook to 260F (125C) or hard-ball stage. Remove from heat and pour quickly *without scraping* onto marble or cold baking sheet. Let stand undisturbed until bubbles no longer rise to the surface of the candy; this will only take a few minutes. Using a spatula, gently turn the edges into the center of the hot candy (this will soften the edges).

When candy is cool enough to handle, pour flavoring and food color over the surface. Butter fingers liberally. Form candy into a ball, then begin stretching and pulling as for taffy. Continue pulling and stretching until candy becomes porous and satiny. *Parallel ridges will form and candy will look puffy and hold its shape. Threads of candy will form on stretched edges.*

Pull out into a rope about 1/2 inch in diameter. Using buttered scissors, cut candy into little pillows about 3/4 inch long. Store in an airtight container for 24 hours to allow candy to crystallize and mellow. If candy has not crystallized after this time, shake the pieces in powdered sugar, then return them to the airtight container; this will begin the crystallization process. Always store them in airtight containers. Makes about 1-1/2 pounds.

Tips
Buttermints are a little bit tricky to make. Since they contain no corn syrup or milk, they will sugar at the least agitation. Don't scrape the cooking pan or move the marble or baking sheet once the syrup is cooling. If they do turn to sugar, recook the candy with 1 cup water just as you did the first time. Be certain there is no sugar left undissolved in the pan or on the wooden spoon. Don't stir the candy once it reaches a boil.
A marble slab or thoroughly chilled baking sheet is necessary for success.
If you make the entire batch, you may want to have someone help with the pulling.

Variations
For Lemon Buttermints—Use lemon extract and yellow food color.
For Licorice Buttermints—Use licorice flavoring and black food color.
For Holiday Buttermints—At Christmas time, divide the candy in two batches and color half of the mints red and half of them green.

From right to left: Sugared Popcorn (page 126); Shaggy Dogs (page 131); and Chewy Coconut Centers (page 124).

Microwave & Easy Candies

With the popularity of the microwave oven, we feel it is important to include several recipes especially for this appliance. Making candy in the microwave does not always save time, so we have included only those recipes that are truly time-savers. Some of these recipes were developed just for the microwave; others have been adapted from conventional recipes.

As you've probably heard (more than once), each microwave oven cooks a little differently. It is important that you learn the characteristics of your own oven and adjust the recipes accordingly.

You'll notice that some of our easy recipes do not require cooking, and we've found that children especially enjoy making these candies.

No-Fail Fudge

Slightly chewy; totally irresistible!

1 (14-ounce) can sweetened condensed milk
1 (12-ounce) package chocolate pieces
Pinch of salt

1 teaspoon vanilla
1/2 cup chopped nuts, if desired

Butter a 9-inch square baking pan; set aside. In a heavy 2-quart saucepan, or medium-size bowl if using microwave, combine condensed milk, chocolate pieces and salt. Place over low heat and stir with a wooden spoon until chocolate is melted, or microwave on Medium to Medium-Low (50% or less) about 2 minutes or until chocolate is softened. Remove from heat and stir until smooth. Stir in vanilla and nuts. Pour into prepared pan. Refrigerate 2 hours or until firm. Cut into 1-inch squares. Makes 81 pieces.

Layered Peanut Butter-Chocolate Fudge

A delightful blend of two flavor favorites.

1 cup peanut butter chips
1 (14-ounce) can sweetened condensed
  milk, divided

3 tablespoons butter
1 cup semisweet or milk chocolate pieces
2 tablespoons butter

Butter an 8-inch square baking pan; set aside. In a heavy 2-quart saucepan, or medium-size bowl if using microwave, combine peanut butter chips with 1/2 cup of the condensed milk and 3 tablespoons butter. Stir over low heat until chips are melted and mixture is well-blended, or microwave on Medium (50%) about 1 minute or until chips are softened and mixture can be blended together. Pour into prepared pan. Refrigerate while preparing chocolate layer.

In a 1-quart saucepan, or small bowl if using microwave, combine chocolate pieces with remaining condensed milk and 2 tablespoons butter. Stir over low heat until chocolate is melted and mixture is smooth, or microwave on Medium (50%) about 1 minute or until chips are softened and mixture can be blended together. Spread over peanut butter mixture. Refrigerate 2 hours or until firm. Just before serving, cut in 1-inch squares. Store in refrigerator. Makes 64 pieces.

Ice Cream Fudge

Quick, easy—and oh-so-tasty! We're sure you'll want to make this recipe many times. The ice cream flavor can be varied—and chocolate is highly recommended.

1 pound dipping chocolate or chocolate bars, melted
1 cup vanilla ice cream

1/2 cup coarsely chopped nuts
1/2 cup finely chopped nuts

Spoon chocolate into a medium-size bowl. Stir in ice cream and coarsely chopped nuts. Refrigerate until mixture is cool. Form into 1-inch balls and roll in finely chopped nuts. Refrigerate until ready to serve. Makes about 30 pieces.

Fudgels

A cross between fudge and truffles, we (somewhat immodestly) are quite proud of the next six recipes—as we came up with the idea. We truly feel they combine the best of two favorite candies—and they're all very easy to make.

After much experimentation, we've been able to refine our idea into a "formula"—you'll probably notice a similarity in the recipes. We suggest you consider these ideas somewhat basic and let your imagination take over. Have fun and try various colors and flavors of compound coatings, and experiment with extract or oil flavorings and other ingredients. For instance, for a "rocky road" effect, stir in 1 cup of miniature marshmallows to any of the fudgels just before pouring them into the cooling pan.

Before you try fudgels, we'd like to share the results of our research—and taste-tests.

Fudgel Hints
Variations exist between the different manufacturers of compound coatings; some are harder and some are softer. If your fudgels are too hard, try them again with 2 additional tablespoons of evaporated milk; if they are too soft, decrease the evaporated milk by 2 tablespoons.

Equivalents—It is difficult to measure the coatings as purchased as the size of the pieces are not precisely the same. This is why the measurements are given for premelted coatings.

1-1/2 cups melted coating = 1 pound
2-1/2 cups compound coating buttons = 1 pound

On the following pages: pecan-topped Brown Sugar Fudgels (page 120); Lemon Coconut Fudgels (page 120); and Neapolitan Fudgels (page 119).

Chocolate Fudgels

This recipe is so good, it's worth the price of the book.

1 pound (about 2-1/2 cups) milk chocolate-flavored compound coating, melted

1/2 cup evaporated milk
1 cup miniature marshmallows
1 teaspoon vanilla

Butter an 8-inch square baking pan; set aside. Place melted coating in a medium-size bowl. In a 1-quart saucepan, or medium-size bowl if using microwave, combine milk and marshmallows. Place pan over low heat and stir occasionally until marshmallows are melted, or microwave on Medium (50%) about 1 minute or until marshmallows are melted. Using a wooden spoon, stir in vanilla. Pour all at once over melted coating and stir until well-mixed. Scrape into prepared pan. Refrigerate for 1 hour. Cut into 1-inch squares. Store in refrigerator. Makes 64 pieces.

Variation
For Chocolate-Mint—Add 3 drops oil of peppermint along with the vanilla.

Cherry Fudgels

Cherries and chocolate with an almond accent. Yum!

1 pound (about 2-1/2 cups) milk chocolate-flavored compound coating, melted
1/2 cup evaporated milk
2 tablespoons margarine

1/4 cup maraschino cherries, drained and chopped
3/4 teaspoon almond extract
1/2 cup nuts, if desired

Butter an 8-inch square baking pan; set aside. Place melted coating in a medium-size bowl. In a 1-quart saucepan, or medium-size bowl if using microwave, combine milk and margarine. Place pan over low heat and stir occasionally until margarine is melted, or microwave on Medium to Medium-Low (50% or less) about 45 seconds or until margarine is melted. Add cherries, almond extract and nuts and mix well. Pour all at once over melted coating and stir with a wooden spoon until well-mixed. Scrape into prepared pan. Refrigerate for 1 hour. Cut into 1-inch squares. Store in refrigerator. Makes 64 pieces.

Peanut Butter Fudgels

If you like peanut butter, you'll love these.

1 pound (about 2-1/2 cups) white,
  vanilla-flavored compound coating,
  melted
1/2 cup evaporated milk

1 cup miniature marshmallows
2/3 cup peanut butter
1 teaspoon vanilla

Butter an 8-inch square baking pan; set aside. Place melted coating in a medium-size bowl. In a 1-quart saucepan, or medium-size bowl if using microwave, combine milk and marshmallows. Place over low heat and stir occasionally until marshmallows are melted, or microwave on Medium (50%) about 1 minute or until marshmallows are melted. Using a wooden spoon, stir in peanut butter and vanilla. Pour all at once over melted coating and stir until well-mixed. Scrape into prepared pan. Refrigerate for 1 hour. Cut into 1-inch squares. Store in refrigerator. Makes 64 pieces.

Neapolitan Fudgels

This pretty, three-layer version combines pink, white and chocolate-flavored compound coatings. For variety, the pink layer can be flavored with almond, strawberry or raspberry extract.

1/2 pound (about 1-1/4 cups) pink
  compound coating, melted
1/2 pound (about 1-1/4 cups) white,
  vanilla-flavored compound coating,
  melted
1/2 pound (about 1-1/4 cups) chocolate-
  flavored compound coating, melted

3/4 cup evaporated milk, divided
1-1/2 cups miniature marshmallows, divided
1/2 teaspoon almond, strawberry or
  raspberry extract

Butter an 8-inch square baking pan; set aside. Place melted coatings in three separate small bowls. In a 1-quart saucepan, or medium-size bowl if using microwave, combine 1/4 cup milk and 1/2 cup marshmallows. Place pan over low heat and stir occasionally until marshmallows are melted, or microwave on Medium (50%) about 30 seconds or until marshmallows are melted. Add desired extract and stir quickly to combine. Add pink coating and stir quickly until mixture is smooth. Spoon immediately into prepared pan and spread evenly with metal spatula. Repeat with white coating, using 1/4 cup milk and 1/2 cup marshmallows. Spread evenly over pink layer. Repeat with chocolate coating, using remaining milk and marshmallows. Quickly spread over white layer. Refrigerate until firm, 15 to 20 minutes. Cut into 1-inch squares. Store in refrigerator. Makes 64 pieces.

Lemon Coconut Fudgels

A light, refreshing summer candy.

1 cup flaked coconut, divided
1/2 pound (about 1-1/4 cups) white,
 vanilla-flavored compound coating,
 melted
1/2 pound (about 1-1/4 cups) yellow
 compound coating, melted

1/2 cup evaporated milk
1 cup miniature marshmallows
1 teaspoon lemon extract

Butter an 8-inch square baking pan; sprinkle 1/2 cup coconut evenly over bottom and set aside. Combine melted coatings in a medium-size bowl. In a 1-quart saucepan, or medium-size bowl if using microwave, combine milk and marshmallows. Place pan over low heat and stir occasionally until marshmallows are melted, or microwave on Medium (50%) about 1 minute or until marshmallows are melted. Using a wooden spoon, stir in lemon extract. Pour all at once over melted coating and stir until well-mixed. Scrape into prepared pan. Sprinkle with remaining coconut. Refrigerate for 1 hour. Cut into 1-inch squares. Store in refrigerator. Makes 64 pieces.

Brown Sugar Fudgels

The family's favorite fudgel.

1 pound (about 2-1/2 cups) white,
 vanilla-flavored compound coating,
 melted
1 cup firmly packed brown sugar
1/2 cup evaporated milk

1 tablespoon butter
1 cup miniature marshmallows
1 teaspoon vanilla
1 cup nuts, if desired

Butter an 8-inch square baking pan; set aside. Place melted coating in a medium-size bowl. In a 1-quart saucepan, or medium-size bowl if using microwave, combine brown sugar, milk and butter. Place pan over low heat and stir occasionally until sugar is dissolved, or microwave on Medium (50%) 2-1/2 to 3 minutes or until sugar is dissolved. Add marshmallows and stir until melted. Add vanilla and nuts. Pour all at once over melted coating and stir until well-mixed. Scrape into prepared pan. Refrigerate for 1 hour. Cut into 1-inch squares. Store in refrigerator. Makes 64 pieces.

Cream Cheese Mints

These easy-to-make mints will make a hit at a party. At Christmas time, divide mixture in half and tint with red and green food color. To intensify colors, roll balls in red and green sugar granules.

1 cup (scant) granulated sugar
1 (3-ounce) package cream cheese, at room
   temperature

1 teaspoon mint extract
1 teaspoon food color
3 cups powdered sugar

Line a baking sheet with waxed paper; set aside. Pour granulated sugar in small bowl and set aside. In another small bowl, combine cream cheese, extract and food color. Stir with a wooden spoon. Gradually add powdered sugar and stir until well-blended. *Mixture will become quite stiff and may require kneading as one would for dough.* When well-mixed, form into balls about 1 inch in diameter. Roll balls in granulated sugar. Place on baking sheet and press flat with the tines of a fork. Refrigerate until ready to serve. Makes 1-1/2 pounds.

Variation
Press ball into a small candy mold and pop out quickly.

Potato-Coconut Candy

Use leftover potatoes for this one.

3/4 cup mashed potatoes
1 (1-pound) box powdered sugar
4 cups shredded coconut
1 teaspoon almond extract

75 whole almonds (about 3/4 cup), roasted
Tempered dipping chocolate (pages
  146-153), if desired

Line a 15″ x 10″ jellyroll pan with waxed paper; set aside. In a large bowl, combine potatoes, sugar, coconut and almond extract. Stir with a wooden spoon or knead with hands until well-mixed. Shape into ovals the size of a walnut. Press an almond into each piece. Serve plain, or dip partially or completely in tempered chocolate. Store in refrigerator. Makes about 75 pieces.

Sour Cream Nuts

In addition to pecans, try almonds or walnuts—or a combination.

1 cup firmly packed brown sugar
1/2 cup granulated sugar
1/2 cup dairy sour cream

1 teaspoon vanilla
3 cups pecan halves

Line a 15″ x 10″ jellyroll pan with waxed paper; set aside. In a heavy 2-quart saucepan, combine sugars with sour cream. Place over medium heat and stir constantly with a wooden spoon until mixture comes to a boil. If sugar crystals are present, wash down sides of the pan with a wet pastry brush.

Clip on candy thermometer. Cook mixture to 238F (115C) or soft-ball stage. Remove from heat and let stand 4 minutes. Stir in vanilla and pecans and mix until well-coated. Turn onto waxed paper-lined pan. Makes 4 cups.

Easy Pralines

Pudding mix eliminates the time-consuming step of caramelizing the sugar, and these candies taste just like traditional pralines.

2/3 cup evaporated milk
1 (3-5/8-ounce) package regular butterscotch
   pudding
1 cup granulated sugar

1/2 cup firmly packed brown sugar
1 tablespoon butter or margarine
1 cup pecans

Line a 15″ x 10″ jellyroll pan with waxed paper; set aside. In a heavy 2-quart saucepan, combine milk, pudding mix, sugars and butter. Place over medium heat and stir with a wooden spoon until mixture comes to a boil. If sugar crystals are present, wash down sides of the pan with a wet pastry brush.

   Clip on candy thermometer. Cook mixture to 234F (115C) or soft-ball stage. Remove from heat. Add pecans and stir until mixture becomes creamy. Drop by spoon onto waxed paper to form 2-inch patties. Cool at room temperature. Store in airtight containers. Makes 15 patties.

Variation
For Easy Chocolate Pralines—Use chocolate pudding mix in place of butterscotch.

Christmas Walnuts

Leave the food color out and make these deliciously coated nuts any time of the year.

1/2 cup water
2 tablespoons light corn syrup
1 cup sugar
1/4 teaspoon salt

1-1/3 cups miniature marshmallows
1/2 teaspoon peppermint extract
Red and green food color
3 cups walnut halves, divided

Butter two 15″ x 10″ jellyroll pans or large trays; set aside. Set aside 2 medium-size bowls. In a 2-quart saucepan, combine water, corn syrup, sugar and salt. Place over high heat and stir with a wooden spoon until mixture comes to a boil. If sugar crystals are present, wash down sides of pan with a wet pastry brush.

   Clip on candy thermometer. Cook syrup to 238F (115C) or soft-ball stage. Remove from heat. Add marshmallows and stir until melted. Add peppermint extract and mix well. Divide mixture evenly between the 2 bowls. Stir red color into one and green color into the other. Add 1-1/2 cups walnuts to each mixture and stir until well-coated. Turn onto baking sheets and separate nuts with 2 forks. Allow to cool at room temperature. Store in airtight containers. Makes 4 cups.

Peanut Butter Chews

No cooking makes these a fast, easy treat.

1/2 cup peanut butter	2/3 cup powdered sugar
1/2 cup corn syrup	About 1 cup nonfat dry milk

In a medium-size bowl, combine peanut butter and corn syrup. Gradually add powdered sugar and stir with a wooden spoon until smooth. Add dry milk a little at a time and stir until mixture is stiff enough to work with your hands. Roll into a long rope 1/2 inch thick. Cut with scissors or a knife into 1-1/2-inch pieces. Store in an airtight container in refrigerator. Makes about 25 pieces.

Chewy Coconut Centers

Fresh marshmallows work best.

1/2 cup light corn syrup	1 teaspoon vanilla
12 large marshmallows	1/4 teaspoon almond extract
1-3/4 cups coconut	Tempered dipping chocolate (pages 146-153)

Line a 15″ x 10″ jellyroll pan with waxed paper; set aside. In a heavy 2-quart saucepan, combine corn syrup and marshmallows. Place over medium heat and stir with a wooden spoon until marshmallows are melted, or microwave on Medium (50%) about 1 minute or until marshmallows are melted. Remove from heat (or microwave) and, using a wooden spoon, stir in coconut, vanilla and almond extract. Refrigerate 10 minutes or until mixture is cool enough to handle.

Butter hands. Shape mixture into small walnut-size balls. Place on baking sheet, flattening each ball slightly. When cool, dip partially or completely in chocolate. Makes about 50 centers.

Variation
Press a roasted almond into each ball.

Chewy Chocolate Rolls

Powdered milk make these a more nutritious snack than most candies.

3 tablespoon margarine
2 (1-ounce) squares unsweetened baking
  chocolate
3 cups powdered sugar

3/4 cup nonfat dry milk
1/2 cup light corn syrup
1/2 teaspoon vanilla

In a 2-quart saucepan, or medium-size bowl if using microwave, combine margarine and chocolate. Place over low heat and stir with a wooden spoon until chocolate is melted, or microwave on Medium to Medium-Low (50% or less) about 2 minutes or until ingredients are softened. Remove from heat (or microwave) and, using a wooden spoon, stir in powdered sugar, dry milk, corn syrup and vanilla. Knead with hands until well-mixed and smooth. Form into a long rope approximately 1/2 inch thick. With a sharp knife, cut into 1-1/2-inch pieces. Wrap in squares of waxed paper or plastic wrap. Makes about 50 pieces.

Chewy Coconut Bars

Reminds you of the store-bought candy bar.

2 cups light corn syrup
1/4 cup butter
1 cup sugar
1 teaspoon salt

1 teaspoon almond extract
1 (14-ounce) package flaked coconut
Tempered dipping chocolate (pages 146-153)

Butter a 9-inch square baking pan; set aside. In a heavy 2-quart saucepan, combine corn syrup, butter, sugar and salt. Place over high heat and stir with a wooden spoon until mixture comes to a boil. Clip on candy thermometer. Cook to 242F (120C) or soft-ball stage. Remove from heat and quickly stir in almond extract and coconut. When well-mixed, scrape into prepared pan. Refrigerate until firm. Cut into 1-inch squares and dip in tempered chocolate. Makes 81 pieces.

Variation
Add 1 cup chopped roasted almonds along with coconut.
Pour a thin layer of caramel over top of uncut coconut mixture. When set, cut into pieces and dip completely in tempered chocolate (pages 146-153).

Marshmallow Popcorn

A simple recipe for children to make.

**2 quarts unbuttered, unsalted popped
  popcorn**
1 cup firmly packed brown sugar

1/2 cup margarine
16 large marshmallows

Butter a 15″ x 10″ baking sheet; set aside. Place popcorn in a large bowl and set aside. In a medium-size glass bowl, combine brown sugar and margarine. Microwave on High (100%) 2 minutes; stir well. Continue microwaving on High about 3 minutes or until sugar is dissolved. Add marshmallows and microwave on High 2 minutes. Stir with a wooden spoon. Return to oven, if needed, and microwave just until marshmallows are melted—the mixture will look foamy. Pour over popcorn and stir with a wooden spoon until popcorn is well-coated. Spread on baking sheet. Makes 10 cups.

Sugared Popcorn

For many, this will bring back childhood memories. To make a colorful popcorn potpourri, divide the syrup in several portions and quickly stir a different color into each one.

6 quarts unbuttered, unsalted popped corn
1/2 cup water
1/4 cup butter or margarine
2 cups sugar

1/2 teaspoon salt
1 teaspoon vanilla
About 3 drops food color

Place popcorn in a large bowl; set aside. In a heavy 2-quart saucepan, combine water, butter, sugar and salt. Place over high heat and stir with a wooden spoon until mixture comes to a boil. If sugar crystals are present, wash down sides of pan with a wet pastry brush. Boil 4 minutes. Remove from heat. Gently stir in vanilla and food color. Pour over popcorn and stir until well-coated. Store in an airtight container. Makes 6 quarts.

Popcorn Cake

A change from the usual birthday cake. Add lollipops or balloons for a colorful, festive touch. (Any extra "cake" can be shaped into popcorn balls.)

8 quarts unbuttered, unsalted popped
    popcorn
1 cup margarine
1/2 cup light corn syrup
2 cups firmly packed brown sugar
1 teaspoon vanilla

1 cup roasted peanuts
1 cup candy-coated chocolate candies
1 cup small gum drops
Assorted decorations such as additional
    candies, marzipan fruits, lollipops, piped
    icing and balloons

Place popped corn in a very large bowl. Set aside a 2-piece ungreased angel food cake pan. In a heavy 2-quart saucepan, combine margarine, corn syrup and sugar. Place over medium heat and stir with a wooden spoon until mixture comes to a boil. Boil 1 minute. Remove from heat and stir in vanilla.

Pour hot syrup over popped corn and stir with a wooden spoon until corn is well-coated. Allow mixture to cool slightly. Stir in nuts and candies. Pack into angel food pan. Cover lightly and allow to cool at room temperature overnight. Remove bottom of pan and turn popcorn cake out onto serving plate or tray. Decorate as desired with assorted candies, icing and balloons. Slice and serve as a regular cake. Serves 12 generously.

Cream 'n Honey Popcorn Balls

If the peanuts and coconut are layered on top of the popcorn, it will mix better.

10 quarts unbuttered, unsalted popped
  popcorn
1 cup peanuts
1/2 cup coconut
1-1/4 cups light, mild honey

1 cup whipping cream
2-1/2 cups sugar
1/2 teaspoon baking soda
1 teaspoon vanilla

In a large bowl, place popcorn, peanuts and coconut; *do not mix.* Set aside. In a heavy 2-quart saucepan, combine honey, cream and sugar. Place over low heat and stir with a wooden spoon until mixture comes to a boil. If sugar crystals are present, wash down sides of pan with a wet pastry brush.

    Clip on candy thermometer. Cook mixture to 245F (120C) or firm-ball stage. Remove from heat; vigorously stir in baking soda. Stir in vanilla. Quickly pour over popcorn and stir to coat thoroughly. Moisten hands with cold water and form mixture into balls. Wrap immediately in waxed paper to hold ball together until cool. Makes about 50 balls.

Easy Caramel Corn

Use 3 quarts of popcorn if you like a heavy coating of syrup, 4 if you like a lighter touch.

3 to 4 quarts unbuttered, unsalted popped
  popcorn
1/2 cup dark corn syrup

1 tablespoon water
1/4 cup butter
1 cup sugar

Place popcorn in a very large bowl; set aside. Combine all remaining ingredients in a 2-quart saucepan. Place over medium-high heat and, stirring constantly with a wooden spoon, bring mixture to a rolling boil. Pour syrup over popcorn and stir to coat well. Makes 3 to 4 quarts.

Microwave Caramel Corn

My friend Carol thought this recipe would round out our popcorn collection.

6 quarts unbuttered, unsalted popped
  popcorn
1/2 cup (1/4 pound) butter or margarine
1/2 cup sweetened condensed milk

1/2 cup light corn syrup
1/2 cup firmly packed brown sugar
1/2 cup granulated sugar
1 teaspoon vanilla

Place popcorn in a very large bowl; set aside. Place butter in a 2-quart glass bowl. Cover with paper towel or waxed paper. Microwave on Medium-High (70%) 30 to 45 seconds or until butter is melted. Remove from oven and add condensed milk, corn syrup and sugars. Stir well with a wooden spoon. Microwave on High (100%) for 7 minutes, stirring several times. Remove from oven and stir in vanilla. Pour syrup over popcorn and stir to coat well. Makes 6 quarts.

Noodle Candy

Kids love to make—and eat—this long-time favorite. The microwave is ideal for melting the chocolate and butterscotch pieces.

1 (6-ounce) package chocolate pieces
1 (6-ounce) package butterscotch pieces

1 (3-ounce) can chow mein noodles

Line a 15″ x 10″ jellyroll pan with waxed paper; set aside. In a 2-quart saucepan, combine chocolate and butterscotch pieces. Place over low heat and stir constantly with a wooden spoon until chocolate and butterscotch are melted and well-mixed. Add noodles and stir until well-coated. Spoon in small clusters onto waxed paper. Cool at room temperature. Lift from waxed paper and store in airtight containers. Makes 24 small clusters.

Variations
Use peanut butter chips in place of butterscotch chips.
Add 1/2 cup peanuts or cashews along with noodles.
Use all chocolate or all butterscotch pieces.

Shaggy Dogs

Keep this dandy candy handy!

2 cups coconut
1/2 cup margarine
1 (6-ounce) package semisweet chocolate
  pieces
2 eggs, beaten

1 (10-ounce) package miniature
  marshmallows
2 cups powdered sugar
1 cup chopped nuts

Sprinkle coconut on large piece of waxed paper or on baking sheet; set aside. In a 2-quart saucepan, or medium-size bowl if using microwave, combine margarine and chocolate pieces. Place pan over low heat and stir occasionally until ingredients are melted, or microwave on Medium (50%) 1 to 1-1/2 minutes until ingredients are softened. Remove from heat (or microwave) and, using a wooden spoon, stir in eggs until well-mixed. Stir in marshmallows, powdered sugar and nuts. Refrigerate briefly until mixture is easy to form.

Shape into logs approximately 1-1/2″ x 5″. Roll each log in coconut. Wrap individually in waxed paper or plastic wrap and refrigerate until firm. To serve, slice into pieces about 1/2 inch thick. Store in refrigerator up to 3 weeks. Makes about 10 logs.

Variation
Use 1/2 cup evaporated milk in place of eggs.

Quick Peanut Butter Treats

Kids love making these candies.

6 cups crisp rice cereal
1 cup light corn syrup
1 cup sugar

1 cup peanut butter
1 teaspoon vanilla

Butter a 9″ x 13″ baking pan; set aside. Place cereal in a large bowl. Combine corn syrup and sugar in a 2-quart saucepan, or medium-size bowl if using microwave. Place pan over medium heat and stir constantly with a wooden spoon until mixture comes to a boil, or microwave on High (100%), stirring several times, about 2 minutes or until mixture boils. Remove from heat (or microwave) and stir in peanut butter and vanilla. Pour over cereal and stir until well-coated. Turn into prepared pan. Moisten one hand with cold water and press mixture firmly into pan. Refrigerate 2 hours or until firm. Cut into 1-1/2-inch squares. Makes about 40 pieces.

Variation
Spread top with tempered dipping chocolate (pages 146-150) before cutting.

Nola's Candy

A melt-in-your-mouth favorite. Usually chocolate centers or balls should be at room temperature for dipping, but this candy is so soft it must be dipped frozen. This causes the chocolate to be dull, but it is not noticeable because of the nut coating.

1 (14-ounce) can sweetened condensed milk
1/2 cup butter, room temperature
1 teaspoon vanilla
2 pounds powdered sugar

Cornstarch
About 3 pounds dipping chocolate, melted
  (pages 146-148)
1 pound roasted almonds, chopped

In a medium-size bowl, combine condensed milk and butter. Beat with an electric mixer until well-blended. Add vanilla. Gradually add powdered sugar and continue beating; if mixture becomes too stiff for mixer, you may have to stir with a wooden spoon. Place bowl in freezer to chill 30 minutes.

After 30 minutes, remove bowl from freezer. Dust hands lightly with cornstarch and form mixture into balls about 3/4 inch in diameter. Place the balls in a clean bowl and freeze 3 hours or until firm. Dip balls *while still frozen* in tempered chocolate. As soon as balls are dipped in chocolate, cover them with chopped almonds. Makes about 150 pieces.

Variations
After powdered sugar has been added, mix in 1 cup shredded coconut.
After powdered sugar has been added, mix in 1 cup chopped nuts.
Add 1/2 cup caramel ice cream topping with condensed milk and butter.

Mint Sandwiches (page 143).

Molded Candies & Compound Coatings

Molded candies are one of the newest and most exciting sweets. They take no cooking and little equipment or experience to make—all very good reasons why many people enjoy creating these colorful confections.

The basis for molded candies is compound coating. It is made from a vegetable oil base and contains sugar, milk solids, emulsifiers, flavoring and color. The vegetable oil base, rather than cocoa butter, makes compound coatings easier to handle—and also less expensive—than dipping chocolate.

There are many different names for compound coating: confectionery coating, summer coating, bon bon coating, Rainbow wafers, almond bark, white chocolate (this is a misnomer), Ice Caps, Pastels, Smooth-'n-Melty and molding chocolate, to name a few. A variety of flavors and colors are available, too. Just be certain you know what flavor you are buying; it can be easy to purchase lime-flavored green wafers when you think you are buying mint-flavored.

Compound coatings are a good choice for hot weather dipping as they are not as affected by excess heat as is dipping chocolate.

This kind of coating can be used for a variety of items—from molding Easter bunnies and Santas to making nut clusters and dipping fresh fruits. While the handling is easier, and the price lower, remember that you will not get top-quality candies by substituting compound coating for dipping chocolate.

The first color in the mold becomes the top of the candy. Using the butterfly as an example, fill in the center of the mold first; a brush works best for small details, and a spoon can be used for larger areas. Tap the mold on the counter top as you go to remove air bubbles, and keep checking the underside of the mold to make sure you like the results; if not, you can add, or carefully subtract, compound coating.

Before adding more colors, be sure that the first layer of compound coating is completely dry. It is also important that the coating is thoroughly dry in the mold before it is removed; otherwise, the finish tends to be a bit dull rather than shiny.

Making molded candies is just the beginning of what you can do with compound coatings. You can dip with it as if it were dipping chocolate; it even comes in chocolate flavors. The finished product is not as good as dipping chocolate but, for a beginner, it is a good learning tool.

Compound coatings are also used to "grain" some of our quick fudge recipes. When using it, you don't have to beat the fudge and you get a terrific texture and flavor. You can even team chocolate-flavored coating with green mint-flavored to make intriguing mint sandwich squares.

We highly recommend that you try your hand at molding; you will have success the very first time—and a lot of fun in the process.

USING COMPOUND COATING

Molds—Purchase shiny plastic molds—either clear for compound coatings, or opaque for hard candy and compound coatings. Wash in warm water and dry thoroughly before using the first time. It is not necessary to wash them after each use unless some coating remains in the mold. Detergents will dry out the plastic and make the candy hard to release. Never put them in the dishwasher; this will damage the molds and warp them.

Store the molds either flat or on one edge. If you store them in a bent position, the molds will be permanently warped. Spraying or greasing the molds is not recommended as this will ruin the finish on the molded items.

Brushes—Brushes are used to paint the melted coatings into the cavities of the mold. Choose brushes specifically designed for this purpose. They have a plastic handle, no metal, and bristles that do not come out. They can be purchased from hobby stores, or check our supplier list on page 155.

Toothpicks can also be used, but it takes considerably more time and patience. They are used for small details such as eyes, lips and other delicate designs.

Melting compound coating—Melting compound coating is much the same as melting chocolate. Use any of the methods described in the chapter on chocolate melting (see page 148). When melting small amounts of several colors, place each color in separate cavities of a muffin tin and place in a low oven, or in 1 inch of water in an electric frying pan turned on low.

You can also melt individual colors in custard cups placed in water in an electric frying pan. Do not allow the water to steam as the moisture will cause the coatings to stiffen and make them unusable. The microwave, on a medium or low setting, also works well.

Flavorings & colorings—When working with compound coating, always use *oil flavorings* rather than extracts. The alcohol and water in the extracts will stiffen the coating. One drop for each cup of coating is all that is required. Paste colors or, preferably, powdered food colors should be used; liquid colors will also cause the coating to stiffen and make it unusable.

Paste and powdered colors are available at most hobby stores, or check the supplier list on page 155. When coloring dark colors, it takes about 1 teaspoon of powdered color for each 1/2 cup of melted coating. If you want a deep red, start with pink compound coating and add powdered red color to obtain the desired shade.

Some coating manufacturers make such a wide variety of colors that it is not necessary to add more color. The various colored coatings can be combined to achieve other desired colors, too.

Painting molds—Place melted coatings on a heating pad or on a warming tray to keep them melted. Using toothpicks, paint on the small details. Remember that whatever you paint first will be on the top, i.e. when doing eyes, paint the colored part on first, then when the first color is dry, add the white of the eye. Turn the mold over periodically as you work to get an idea of the appearance of the finished mold. Use brushes to paint on the larger details. When painting over a color, be sure that it is completely dry or the colors will run together. If you make a mistake and get too much coating in the mold, use a clean toothpick to scrape away the excess.

When the coatings are dry, fill the mold cavities with melted coating. Do this with a spoon or, if you are doing a large number of molds, you may want to place the melted coating in a squeeze bottle. After the molds have been filled, lightly tap the mold on a countertop to release any air bubbles that may be trapped. Next, place the mold in the freezer for about 10 minutes or until the coating has hardened. Release the molds and store them in airtight containers in a cool place.

Any leftover compound coatings can be reused. Scrape the excess onto waxed paper and allow it to harden. Store in airtight containers in a cool place.

Three-Dimensional Molds

Hollow Molds—If you are going to paint the mold, paint each half separately. When painted colors have hardened, continue as follows:

In one-half of a 2-piece mold, fill 1/2-full of melted coating. Place the other half of mold over coating.

Clip the 2 pieces of mold together with bulldog clips (available at office suppliers). Rotate the mold to coat both sides. Place the mold in the freezer for about 2 minutes. Remove from the freezer and rotate mold again, recoating the inside of the mold. Place in freezer for 2 more minutes. Remove and rotate again. Place in freezer again, upside-down, for 2 minutes.

Remove from freezer and lift off 1 side of the mold, then the other. Trim off excess coating from seam with a sharp knife. You may want to use clean cotton gloves to hold the candy; too much handling with warm hands can leave fingerprints or even melt the surface of the molded candy.

Solid Molds—Using a 2-piece mold, fill one side of the mold to within 1/8 inch of the top. Fill the other half of the mold all the way to the top. Place in freezer for about 20 minutes. Remove from freezer and fill the small half completely with melted coating. Place the other half over the top of the melted coating, making sure the mold is properly lined up, and firmly press the two halves together. Secure with bulldog clips. Lay the mold flat in the freezer for 5 to 10 minutes. Remove from freezer and lift off 1 side of the mold, then the other. Trim off excess coating from seam with a sharp knife.

Covered Leaves—Pick fresh nonpoisonous leaves, such as rose, citrus or camellia. Wash and dry thoroughly. Brush on a thin layer of melted coating on underside of leaves. Place coating-side up on a baking sheet and set in freezer for about 1 minute. Remove from freezer and carefully peel off leaf. Store in a cool place.

Compound Coating Ideas

Glazed Apricots—Dip glazed apricot half-way in melted compound coating. Arrange on waxed paper-lined tray and place in refrigerator until set, about 5 minutes. This makes a tasty as well as very attractive candy.

Dipped Pineapple—Dip glazed or candied pineapple half-way in melted compound coating. Arrange on waxed-paper lined tray and place in refrigerator until set, about 2 minutes. Try different colors and flavors of coating.

Nut Clusters—Mix equal amounts of melted coating and roasted nuts in a small bowl. Stir with a spoon until mixed. Drop on waxed paper-lined trays. Place in refrigerator until hard. Store in a cool place. Use your favorite nuts or a combination of nuts.

Easter Nests—Use equal amounts of melted green compound coating and shredded coconut. Combine in a small bowl and stir with a spoon. Add more coconut if mixture seems too soft. Spoon onto waxed paper-lined trays and make a depression in each nest with the back of the spoon. While coating is still wet, press in small jelly beans. Place in refrigerator until hard. Store in a cool place.

Pretzels—Using a fork, dip your favorite size and shape of pretzels in melted coating. Arrange in a single row on waxed paper-lined trays. Place in refrigerator until hard. Store in a cool place. You can make these weeks in advance of serving.

MARZIPAN

Marzipan is an almond-flavored confection of European origin, and the miniature fruits and vegetables into which marzipan is often formed have long been a favorite confection in Europe. It is composed of almond paste, powdered sugar and either egg white or margarine; corn syrup or marshmallow creme and flavorings are also added.

You can make your own almond paste, but it is difficult to get it smooth enough to use. As you can tell, we believe in starting from scratch with most of our candies, but marzipan is the exception: we suggest you purchase it by the roll or in a can. Marzipan is available in most gourmet sections of supermarkets, or check our supplier list on page 155. You will note that we have included a recipe for almond paste on page 141 if you do choose to make your own.

Marzipan has the texture of modeling clay or a stiff pie dough, and it will keep for several months if stored airtight in the refrigerator. Besides just eating it plain, marzipan is used to decorate cakes and cookies, for table decorations, and as a special treat when you want a different kind of candy. Children love to make this confection and can easily mold fruits, vegetables, cut-outs and little statue-like figures just as they do from clay.

After marzipan is formed, you can paint on it, roll it in colored sugar, powdered cocoa or chocolate shot. Let your imagination run wild and you will be surprised at the amazing things that you can do with this confection. Instead of miniature fruits, make life-sized fruits for an edible centerpiece. For the holidays, decorate fruitcakes with holly and berries made of marzipan.

Since you don't even have to cook the commercial almond paste, there is no question of your having success with it. Start a family tradition: assemble the supplies and have everyone create "marzipan art" together.

Flavoring Marzipan—In Europe, lemon juice, rose water or orange-flavored liqueur is often used to flavor marzipan. In the United States, vanilla, rum, cherry or almond extracts are popular.

Equipment and Tools—Canapé cutters, small cookie cutters, toothpicks, orange sticks, a flat grater, at least 2 clean watercolor brushes, food color, small dishes and waxed paper-lined trays are the main tools needed for marzipan figures.

Shaping Marzipan—When you are ready to shape the marzipan, decide what shapes and colors you are going to make. Divide the dough into small portions and color each with 1 to 2 drops of food color. With your hands, mix each color separately. If the dough becomes too dry, add a drop of water or light corn syrup and mix thoroughly.

As each shape is formed, place on waxed paper-lined tray. Be sure sides of items do not touch so that each may dry evenly.

Tinting and Shading Marzipan—In order to appear more lifelike, some fruits and vegetables will require additional tinting and shading. In a small dish, place 3 tablepoons water and 2 to 3 drops food color. Mix thoroughly. To color large areas, such as the blush of a peach, use a small clean piece of cloth. Dip it into the colored water and apply to fruit. For small areas and details such as dots and stripes, use a small watercolor brush.

Glazing Marzipan—Glazing is used to add a shine to the marzipan and to keep it soft and fresh. Apply glaze with a small watercolor brush.

Glaze

After forming and shading marzipan, allow figures to dry on waxed paper-lined trays for 2 hours at room temperature before applying glaze.

3 tablespoons light corn syrup
1 tablespoon hot water

Mix ingredients thoroughly in a small bowl. Apply to marzipan with a small brush. Allow to dry completely before storing.

Marshmallow Creme Marzipan

This is our favorite marzipan.

7 to 8 ounces almond paste
1/4 cup margarine, at room temperature
1 tablespoon light corn syrup

1/3 cup marshmallow creme
1/2 teaspoon vanilla
About 3 cups powdered sugar, sifted

In a large bowl, break up almond paste with a fork. Add margarine, corn syrup, marshmallow creme and vanilla. Work mixture with hands until smooth. Add powdered sugar 1 cup at a time, kneading with hands until mixture is the consistency of stiff pie dough. If mixture becomes too stiff and dry, add about 1 teaspoon water and knead until mixture is pliable. You may use immediately, or wrap airtight and keep refrigerated for several months. Before using, bring to room temperature and knead until soft and pliable. Makes 25 to 30 small fruits.

Variation
Use rum, cherry or almond extract in place of vanilla.

On the following pages: Marzipan "produce stand" (pages 136-141).

THE (ENDLESS) POSSIBILITIES WITH MARZIPAN

Apples	Use light green dough with a little yellow added. Form into balls. Cut out leaves using green dough (or use purchased leaves). Attach with corn syrup.
Apricots or Peaches	Use orange and pink dough. Form into balls and make a crease on one side. Use the end of the paint brush handle to indent one end. They will be shaded later.
Bananas	Use yellow dough. Shape to resemble a banana. Brown stripes or speckles and green ends are added later.
Cherries	Use deep red dough. Shape into balls. Group two together, add stems, if desired, and 1 leaf and attach with corn syrup.
Grapes	Use pale yellow, green or purple dough. Form little round balls and arrange in clusters. Cut out leaves using green dough (or use purchased leaves). Attach with a drop of corn syrup.
Leaves	Use green dough. (Leaves may also be purchased.)
Lemons	Use pale yellow dough. Roll over fine grater for texture. Press a whole clove in the stem end.
Oranges	Use orange dough. Roll over fine grater for texture. Press a whole clove in the stem end.
Pears	Use light green or yellow dough. Press a whole clove in the stem end. Pears need shading with additional colors.
Strawberries	Use red dough. Roll on fine grater for texture, or roll in red sugar purchased in small bottles from the supermarket. For strawberry leaves, cut out small star shapes from green marzipan, or use real or purchased leaves. Fasten leaves with a drop of corn syrup.
Carrots	Use orange dough. Add crosswise stripes by making indentations with the side of a toothpick.
Peas in a pod	Use green dough. Form a ball of dough into a flat oval shape. Place 4 or 5 small green peas in center. Fold sides partly inward and pinch ends lightly together.
Potatoes	Use uncolored dough. Shape in an oval, making one end slightly larger than the other. Make eyes with a toothpick. Roll in cocoa, brushing off excess with a dry brush. Do not glaze unless you plan to keep them for awhile.
Pumpkins	Use orange dough. Make impressions with the back of a knife. Add a green or brown dough stem at the top.
Squash	Use appropriate color of dough and shape accordingly.

Marzipan can be cut into a variety of shapes with canapé cutters and used to decorate cakes or cookies. Flowers can be made by shaping and flattening small bits of dough into petal shapes. Place on waxed paper-lined trays and add petals in a slightly overlapping pattern, fastening each with a drop of corn syrup. Paint, dry and glaze.

Egg White Marzipan

You may use this immediately, or make it months ahead and store airtight in the refrigerator.

7 to 8 ounces almond paste
2 egg whites, at room temperature

1/2 teaspoon vanilla
About 3 cups powdered sugar, sifted

In a large bowl, break up almond paste with a fork. Add egg whites and vanilla. Work mixture with hands until smooth. Add powdered sugar 1 cup at a time, kneading with hands until mixture is the consistency of stiff pie dough. If mixture becomes too stiff and dry, add about 1 teaspoon water and knead until mixture is pliable. You may use immediately, or wrap airtight and keep refrigerated for several months. Before using, bring to room temperature and knead until soft and pliable. Makes 25 to 30 small fruits.

Variation
Use rum, cherry or almond extract in place of vanilla.

Almond Paste

You must use a food processor to make this recipe.

1 cup blanched raw almonds
1/2 cup sugar

1-1/2 tablepoons water
1 tablespoon lemon juice

In food processor, grind almonds very, very fine; leave in work bowl. In a 1-quart saucepan, combine sugar, water and lemon juice. Cook over medium heat, stirring constantly with a wooden spoon, until the sugar is dissolved and syrup comes to a boil. Remove spoon and boil mixture 3-1/2 minutes.

  With food processor running, carefully pour hot syrup through feed tube into almonds. Run until just blended. Remove paste and form into a ball. Place in a tightly covered container and refrigerate 3 to 4 days to mellow. Makes 11 ounces of almond paste.

Fresh Strawberry Dips

This is our pièce de résistancé cover photograph. Make these when fresh strawberries are available and serve them as a dessert within hours of dipping. They cannot be made in advance and stored.

1/3 pound (about 3/4 cup) pink or white
  compound coating, melted
1/3 pound (about 3/4 cup) chocolate-flavored
  compound coating, melted

10 large fresh strawberries with leaves,
  washed and dried

Line a 9″ x 13″ baking pan with waxed paper; set aside. Place the compound coatings in containers at least 2 inches deep. Holding a strawberry at the fullest part of the berry, dip 1/2 to 3/4 of the berry in pink coating. Allow excess to drip back into container. Lay berry on waxed paper to allow coating to harden.

When all the berries have been dipped in pink coating and the coating is hard, dip each berry in the chocolate coating to cover about 2/3 of the pink coating, creating a 3-color effect. Place on waxed paper to harden. Makes 10.

Candy Pizza

According to Ruth, this rich snack-dessert serves "three teenagers or 26 adults."

2 pounds (about 5 cups) chocolate-flavored
  compound coating, melted
1-1/2 cups crisp rice cereal
1/2 cup chopped nuts

1/2 cup candy-coated chocolate candies
1/2 cup red candied cherries
1/2 cup (2 to 3 ounces) white compound
  coating

Line a 12- or 15-inch pizza pan or large baking sheet with waxed paper. In a medium-size bowl, combine chocolate-flavored coating and cereal. Spread mixture on the waxed paper in a circle 10 to 12 inches in diameter and about 1/2 inch thick. While coating is moist, lightly press nuts, candy pieces and cherries over "crust." Place in refrigerator to harden. Shortly before serving, melt white coating. Remove pizza from refrigerator and drizzle white coating over top. Serve at room temperature. Makes 16 slices.

Mint Sandwiches

These clever little candy sandwiches are attractive, popular—and easy to make. They can be made with dipping chocolate rather than the chocolate-flavored coatings, but the layers tend to separate and be more difficult to handle than when using compound coatings.

2/3 pound (about 1-2/3 cups) milk
   chocolate-flavored compound coating,
   melted

2/3 pound (about 1-2/3 cups) dark
   chocolate-flavored compound coating,
   melted

2/3 pound (about 1-2/3 cups) green
   mint-flavored compound coating, melted

Line a 15″ x 10″ jellyroll pan with waxed paper; set aside.

Pour milk chocolate-flavored coating in center of waxed paper. Using a pancake turner or spatula, spread the coating in a layer about 1/8 inch thick. Allow to stand at room temperature until the coating is just beginning to set up.

Pour green coating over chocolate coating and spread with hands, a pancake turner or spatula until smooth. Allow to stand until the coating is just beginning to set up. Pour dark chocolate-flavored coating over the green layer and spread with hands, a pancake turner or spatula to make a smooth finish. Allow to set up at room temperature until firm.

To serve, remove candy from pan by lifting waxed paper liner and place on flat cutting surface. Using a long, thin-bladed sharp knife, cut mints into 1-inch squares. Store in a cool area, or in an airtight container in the refrigerator. Makes about 150 sandwiches.

Variation
Use a variety of colors and flavors of compound coatings. For example, white compound coating can be used in place of the green mint-flavored coating. Add any flavor and food color desired.

Barks

Almond bark or peppermint bark are easily made with compound coatings. Simply mix equal amounts of ingredients together. This versatile recipe can be made in small and large amounts and with a variety of nuts and coatings. For example, add crisp rice cereal to melted coating (or melted chocolate) for a crunch-type candy bar.

1 pound (about 2-1/2 cups) compound
   coating, melted

1-1/2 cups chopped nuts, crushed
   peppermint candies and/or crisp rice
   cereal

Line a 15″ x 10″ jellyroll pan or large tray with waxed paper. Place melted coating in a medium-size bowl. Add nuts and candies and mix well. Spread about 1/4 inch thick on waxed paper. Place in refrigerator until hard. Cut or break into serving pieces. Makes about 2 pounds.

Chocolate

The majority of candy lovers love chocolate most of all.

For a bit of background—which might give you even more of an appreciation—chocolate comes from cacao beans, which are grown in a comparatively small area near the Equator on cacao trees. There are many varieties of cacao beans, each with a distinctive flavor and color. Ultimately, each chocolate manufacturer blends the beans to develop the flavor and color desired. The hulls are removed and processed into nibs, which contain cocoa butter and cocoa. This very bitter raw form is pressed into cakes and sold as baking chocolate. The formal name is "chocolate liquor" and this is the base for all chocolate products. When most of the cocoa butter has been removed from the liquor, the remaining product is ground into cocoa powder.

TYPES OF CHOCOLATE

Dipping chocolate—Most dipping chocolate comes in 10-pound blocks, though it can be purchased in smaller quantities at some confectionery supply houses or from candy businesses. Some manufacturers produce dipping chocolate in small flat drops called *buttons*. These are easier to work with, but they do look like some chocolate-flavored compound coatings. Be sure to double-check before purchase.

Semisweet chocolate—This type of chocolate is made by adding both lecithin—an emulsifier to help keep the cocoa butter from separating—and sugar to the chocolate liquor. If the cocoa butter does separate out, the chocolate develops a grayish exterior, which is called "bloom." It does not harm the chocolate in any way except appearance, and once the chocolate is melted, it will return in suspension. Semisweet chocolate is available in 10-pound blocks, 1-ounce squares and morsels, pieces and chips.

Sweet dark chocolate—Without a doubt, this is the favorite of true chocolate-lovers. Similar to semisweet, but with more sugar added, this chocolate is also available in 10-pound blocks, bars and morsels, pieces and chips.

Milk chocolate—Mild in flavor and light in color, this is the most popular form of chocolate. It is a combination of chocolate liquor, sugar, whole milk solids and lecithin. Milk chocolate is available in 10-pound blocks, bars, buttons, morsels, pieces and chips.

Semisweet, sweet and milk chocolates can be mixed and blended at home to produce the flavor and color desired. If you use a high-quality dipping chocolate, you can mix brands and types; don't mix with chocolate pieces or compound coatings, only dipping chocolate.

White chocolate—White chocolate (a misnomer as it does not contain chocolate solids) can be a bit hard to find, but it is well worth the extra effort. Made with a cocoa butter base, milk solids, sugar and lecithin, it has a creamy white color, the aroma of chocolate and a very mild flavor. It makes excellent truffles and can be molded into a variety of novelty items.

Don't confuse white chocolate with white compound coating; there is a world of difference in both flavor and texture. White chocolate is also a little more expensive than dipping chocolate.

Chocolate morsels, pieces or chips—These small drops of chocolate—usually semisweet or milk—are used primarily for baking and candymaking. They often develop "bloom" due to improper storage. This will not harm them and the cocoa butter will return in suspension when the chocolate is heated.

Imitation chocolate pieces or chocolate-flavored chips are made from compound coatings and, to our tastes, are decidedly inferior in flavor. We do not recommend their use in our recipes.

Compound coatings—These coatings go by a variety of *noms de plume:* molding chocolate, almond bark, summer coating, bonbon coating, confectioners coating, Rainbow wafers, Pastels, Smooth-'n-Melty and Ice Caps. As they are made from a vegetable oil base rather than cocoa butter, they are less expensive to purchase than dipping chocolate. A variety of flavors and colors are available including dark and light chocolate.

Compound coating can be used in many recipes as an ingredient, and for making molded and special-occasion candies. While we do not recommend using compound coatings to do all of your dipping, it can be used to help develop your dipping technique; for one, it is much easier to work with than dipping chocolate as there is no cocoa butter to cause streaking.

When purchasing compound coating, make certain you know what you are buying. As it is available in many flavors and colors, "green" can be vanilla, lime or mint. If in doubt, ask for a sample taste.

MELTING CHOCOLATE

There are many ways to melt chocolate. The method you choose will depend on the amount you have to melt as well as the equipment available. Regardless of the method you use, remember these three points: chocolate will scorch if it is heated at a high temperature; it will tighten or lump if it is exposed to any moisture such as steam, and it will absorb odors easily.

In general, any gentle heat source can be used if you remember to keep moisture away, and avoid appliances such as an electric frying pan that may have hot spots.

Before melting chocolate, break it into small pieces with a clean hammer, ice pick or the tip of a sturdy knife. The pieces should be about the size of an egg or smaller, though of course they won't be smooth and round. As you might expect, the smaller the pieces, the faster the chocolate will melt. It is not necessary to grate the chocolate before melting; by the time you have this done, the chocolate could be melted!

Chocolate can be remelted many times as long as there is no moisture present and it hasn't been scorched. If the cocoa butter comes to the surface and blooms, don't worry: it will remelt.

Conventional oven—This is our favorite way to melt chocolate. It is easy and you don't have to worry about moisture. Depending on how much you are going to melt, put the chopped chocolate in a saucepan, baking pan or bowl; a lid is optional. Place it in the oven, set the thermostat to the lowest temperature setting possible, and close the door.

Check every few minutes to make sure that the pan is not getting too hot. To test the temperature, place your bare hand on the side of the pan. If it is too warm to leave there, remove the pan from the oven with hot pads and stir the chocolate until the pan cools. Return the pan to the oven. Most ovens will remain cool enough so that you will not need to remove the pan.

Be sure you stir the chocolate fairly often as it melts. With this method, it should only take about 30 minutes to melt 5 pounds of chocolate. If you find that your oven cannot be turned down low enough, simply turn the oven off after the chocolate has been in for 5 minutes.

Double-boiler—Technically, what we really mean here is "double-simmer." If the water is allowed to boil, steam is produced and released around the chocolate, which will tighten the chocolate and make it unusable for dipping. Place the chocolate in the top part of the double boiler—or other pan that sets above the water level—and add hot water to the lower pan. Set on burner and turn heat to lowest setting. Stir the chocolate frequently and do not allow the water to boil.

We feel that this method takes a lot of time and attention, and we remain partial to the oven method of melting chocolate.

Microwave—Some people have success with the microwave oven, depending on the amount of chocolate you have to melt. If you have more than a few pounds, we recommend you consider another method. Baking chocolate melts well in the microwave, but milk chocolate tends to scorch rather easily. As a general rule, when melting or heating chocolate in the microwave, it is best to use Medium to Medium-Low (50% or less).

Slow cook pot—Place chocolate in the pot, cover with a lid and turn to the lowest setting. Stir the chocolate occasionally and test it with your finger every so often to be sure it isn't getting too hot. If it feels very warm, turn off the pot, remove the lid and allow the chocolate to finish melting from the residual heat.

Pilot light or oven light—If you have a lot of time, place chocolate in a pan in the oven and allow the heat from the pilot light or oven light to melt it. This is a very safe method, but it does take a long time, possibly overnight.

Assorted truffles (pages 46-50)

CHOCOLATE HANDLING

Dipping—Dipping is the process of covering a center, nut or fruit with melted chocolate or compound coating. Years ago, all quality chocolates were hand-dipped; today, most chocolates are machine-dipped or "enrobed." Hand-dipping your own chocolates is the most challenging and rewarding experience in candymaking. It takes much practice to become proficient at dipping—but it is so enjoyable when you do succeed.

Always start with quality chocolate: the better your chocolate, the better your chances for success. Each experienced dipper has his or her own preference. Usually the brand you learn with and have success with is the brand you end up sticking with.

There are several good brands on the market such as Merckens, Peters and Guittard. A good chocolate should have a smooth melt, which means there is no noticeable grain when melted on the tongue. Flavor is also important: if you don't like the taste, you won't like it for dipping.

Most people prefer milk chocolate, as it has a very mild, sweet flavor. Some prefer the sweet dark chocolate, which is especially good on sweet fruit centers or on mints. If you fall somewhere in the middle, chocolate can be mixed at home to produce a blend somewhere between dark and light. As long as you are working with quality chocolate, different brands can be mixed.

By all means, remember this cardinal rule: *Never add anything to the chocolate.* This means paraffin, vegetable oil and the like. Some people feel that the chocolate is easier to handle if it contains some of these extra's. They simply aren't necessary—and these "additives" can literally leave a bad taste in your mouth. Once you get the dipping technique down-pat, you'll prefer using fresh, pure ingredients. One of the benefits of making homemade candy is that you can control exactly what goes into it.

DETERMINING AMOUNT TO BUY

To determine the amount of chocolate you'll need, use this rule of thumb. Begin by figuring out how many pounds of finished chocolates you want. Since chocolate doubles, if you want 20 pounds of chocolates, buy 10 pounds of chocolate. (Most beginners tend to use more chocolate than necessary; as you become experienced, you will find this rule of thumb holds true.)

GETTING ORGANIZED

To set up equipment and ingredients, have the melted chocolate about 18 inches in front of you, the centers or other items to be dipped on your left, an electric frying pan directly in front of you, and trays covered with waxed paper to your right. (If you are left-handed, reverse the trays and centers.) The room should be 62F to 68F (15-20C) and the centers should be room temperature. You can place the pan or bowl of melted chocolate on a heating pad to keep it warm, or occasionally place it in a warm oven to keep chocolate the correct consistency for dipping.

Tempering—To prepare the melted chocolate for dipping, it must be mixed and cooled to the proper temperature. This is called "tempering the chocolate." With the right hand, place three handfuls of melted chocolate into the center of a *cold* electric frying pan. Place your right hand (or left if left-handed) with fingers together and hand slightly cupped at the edge of the chocolate. With cupped hand, make "S" motions through the chocolate. Continue this mixing and cooling process until chocolate feels cool to the touch—about 85F (30C).

To test for the correct temperature, place one finger in the chocolate and touch it to the waxed paper-lined tray. Let this spot stand 3 minutes. While waiting, continue moving the chocolate in the frying pan. If the spot hardens and no longer looks wet after 3 minutes, the chocolate is at the correct temperature for dipping. If it is still wet after 3 minutes, repeat the spot test. If it is still wet, check the temperature of your room; it should be no more than 70F (20C). When chocolate is cool enough to dip, try both of the following methods and choose the one that is easiest for you.

DIPPING CHOCOLATES

The first step in dipping is to break the chocolate into pieces about the size of an egg. It can then be melted in the oven, double-boiler, microwave, slow cook pot, or from the warmth of a pilot light or oven light. We prefer the oven method.

Once the chocolate is melted, we recommend an electric frying pan for "tempering." This mixing-and-dipping technique is very important as it makes the dipping easier and assures the dipped chocolate is glossy. Place 3 handfuls of chocolate in the *cold* frying pan. With the hand slightly cupped, make gentle "S" motions through the chocolate. When the chocolate feels cool, it is ready for dipping. Continue these "S" motions as you dip.

Finger method: This is one of two dipping techniques. Drop the fondant (or other candy) center in the tempered chocolate. Pick up a handful of chocolate and completely cover the fondant.

Next, pick up the dipped chocolate, turn your hand palm-side-up and let excess chocolate drip back into the frying pan. Tapping the back of your hand against the edge of the pan also helps to remove some of the excess chocolate.

Slide your thumb under the dipped chocolate . . .

. . . turn your hand palm-side-down and "flip"/slide the chocolate onto a waxed paper-lined tray. This technique is similar to shooting marbles though, with chocolates, less exuberance is required.

DIPPING CHOCOLATES

Palm method: For this technique, place the palm of one hand in the tempered chocolate. Turn the hand palm-side-up and use the other hand to place the center—in this case, a Caramel Cluster—on the finger tips. Close your hand over the candy.

Open your hand and you should find that the candy is completely covered with tempered chocolate. If it isn't, close your hand and open it again. When the center is completely covered, drop it gently onto a waxed paper-lined tray.

Finger method—Stir chocolate with the fingers of the right hand. With your left hand, place fondant center in middle of chocolate in frying pan. With right hand, pick up a handful of melted chocolate from frying pan and cover the ball of fondant. With right hand, pick up covered fondant. Turn hand palm up and allow excess chocolate to return to frying pan. Tap the back of your hand against the edge of the frying pan to remove excess chocolate. Slide your thumb under the fondant and, turning palm down, slide the chocolate onto a waxed paper-lined tray.

When approximately 1/4 of the original amount of melted chocolate remains in the frying pan, add 2 more handfuls of chocolate from the melting pan. Go through the mixing process with the fresh chocolate, thoroughly incorporating fresh chocolate with the cooler chocolate. Proceed with dipping until once again 1/4 of the chocolate remains in the frying pan. Add fresh chocolate and repeat mixing and dipping until all the centers are covered with chocolate.

If the chocolate in the frying pan begins to harden during the dipping process, turn the heat on in the frying pan for *exactly 2 seconds*. Any longer than 2 seconds will overheat the pan and cause the chocolates to have white streaks on them. Mix the softened chocolate using the "S" motion, and continue dipping the centers.

Palm method—Place the palm of your right hand in the cool chocolate, then turn palm up. With your left hand, pick up a fondant center and place it on the finger tips of your right hand. Close your hand, then open it. The center should be covered with chocolate. If it isn't, close your hand and open it again. When the center is covered, drop it onto the waxed paper-lined tray on your right.

"Signing" Your Chocolates—Undoubtedly you've noticed that good chocolates are given a finishing touch: a signature design on top. This identifies the type of center—and it also covers up your dipping.

At first, you will probably not be able to place a design on the top of your chocolates. Don't be concerned, as this takes much practice. Instead, place a pecan half or whole almond on the chocolate while the chocolate is still wet. You can also sprinkle chocolate shot, chopped nuts or coconut on top, or you might try a "rough dip," which is an easy way to achieve an interesting effect. (With the latter technique, a signature is unnecessary.)

When you become comfortable at dipping, you will want to try to make a mark, or signature, on the top of each chocolate. To do this, after you have placed the dipped chocolate on the waxed paper, lightly tap the top surface of the chocolate with the middle finger of the right hand and pull up a string of chocolate an inch or so long. Guide this string around the top of the chocolate to make the design you desire. If your first attempt is not satisfactory, tap the surface again and repeat the process. Start with straight lines and circles. When you have mastered these, move on to more complicated marks such as stars, bows and letters of the alphabet.

"Rough Dip"—Although a smooth, glossy finish is traditional, you can also create an attractive textured effect on your dipped candies. (See the truffle pictured on page 53.) For this look, as you dip simply mix 1 cup of finely chopped nuts into 1 pound of tempered chocolate.

"Double Dip"—Dip center in tempered milk chocolate (or melted compound coating). When hardened, dip again in milk chocolate or coating or, for the second dip, try dark chocolate (or another color of coating).

A Word of Encouragement—Do not get discouraged the first time you attempt to dip. A lot of practice is necessary to perfect this art. It is easier to do if you have observed someone who knows what they're doing. Check with a local candy store as many of them welcome "watchers."

It takes several hours for the chocolates to dry enough to handle. When thoroughly dry, place in glassine candy cups (the brown papers that professional candies come in— available at confectionery stores listed on page 155) and store in boxes, metal tins or plastic ware. Place waxed paper between the layers to keep the chocolates from getting scratched. Store in a cool area, but not in the refrigerator as the humidity would cause the chocolate to absorb moisture. You can freeze the finished chocolates if you wrap them in moisture-vaporproof containers. After freezing, allow candy to warm to room temperature before unwrapping.

Any melted chocolate that is left in the melting pan or the frying pan can be saved and remelted many times. You may prefer to use the leftover chocolate immediately to make nut or raisin clusters, or to cover marshmallows for a family treat.

CHOCOLATE STORAGE

Chocolate should be stored in a cool place with no moisture present. If you plan to store it longer than a few months, wrap in moisture-vaporproof paper and freeze. Be certain it is airtight or moisture will seep in and ruin the chocolate. When removing chocolates from the freezer, let them stand at room temperature for several hours before unwrapping. This will prevent moisture, in the form of condensation, from forming on the chocolate.

Remember, too, that chocolate will absorb aromas so be sure you keep it away from perfume, smoke and other sources of odor. Chocolate will melt easily from the heat of the sun, so keep this in mind when placing your special candies in the car. If your chocolates do happen to melt, allow them to firm up again. The resulting "bloom" will not be harmful.

"SIGNING" CHOCOLATES

Whether you use the finger or palm method of dipping, as soon as the dipped candy is placed on the waxed paper, use your middle finger and gently tap the top surface of the chocolate several times. This enables you to pull up a string of chocolate about an inch long.

Guide this string around the top of the chocolate, making any kind of design you'd like. As you become proficient with this technique, you will probably want to "label" your chocolates with a particular sign, indicating what the center is—just as professional candymakers do.

Chocolate Dipping Trouble-Shooting Guide

Use this chart as a guideline if your finished chocolates are not as professional-looking as you might have hoped. Symptoms usually will not be apparent until chocolate has set up—several hours after dipping. Take heart, though, as chances are they'll still taste great! (If you don't like cloudy or dull-appearing chocolates, wrap them in foil squares and no one will be the wiser.)

Dipped Chocolate Appearance:

Bottom	Top	Caused By:	Remedy:
cloudy	cloudy	coating too cold	increase temperature
dull	dull	coating not tempered	work coating between each dip
shiny	cloudy	coating too hot	decrease temperature
cloudy	luster with dull spots	coating too hot	cool coating and work between each dip
wet & sticky	wet & sticky	coating much too hot	cool and work more before dipping
cloudy	dull	cooled too slowly	decrease room temperature
looks good 1st day, cloudy second day	looks good 1st day, cloudy second day	cooled too slowly	decrease room temperature and cool where air can circulate

Metric Chart

Comparison to Metric Measure

When You Know	Symbol	Multiply By	To Find	Symbol
teaspoons	tsp	5.0	milliliters	ml
tablespoons	tbsp	15.0	milliliters	ml
fluid ounces	fl. oz.	30.0	milliliters	ml
cups	c	0.24	liters	l
pints	pt.	0.47	liters	l

When You Know	Symbol	Multiply By	To Find	Symbol
quarts	qt.	0.95	liters	l
ounces	oz.	28.0	grams	g
pounds	lb.	0.45	kilograms	kg
Fahrenheit	F	5/9 (after subtracting 32)	Celsius	C

Liquid Measure to Milliliters

1/4 teaspoon	=	1.25 milliliters
1/2 teaspoon	=	2.5 milliliters
3/4 teaspoon	=	3.75 milliliters
1 teaspoon	=	5.0 milliliters
1-1/4 teaspoons	=	6.25 milliliters
1-1/2 teaspoons	=	7.5 milliliters
1-3/4 teaspoons	=	8.75 milliliters
2 teaspoons	=	10.0 milliliters
1 tablespoon	=	15.0 milliliters
2 tablespoons	=	30.0 milliliters

Fahrenheit to Celsius

F	C
200—205	95
220—225	105
245—250	120
275	135
300—305	150
325—330	165
345—350	175
370—375	190
400—405	205
425—430	220
445—450	230
470—475	245
500	260

Liquid Measure to Liters

1/4 cup	=	0.06 liters
1/2 cup	=	0.12 liters
3/4 cup	=	0.18 liters
1 cup	=	0.24 liters
1-1/4 cups	=	0.3 liters
1-1/2 cups	=	0.36 liters
2 cups	=	0.48 liters
2-1/2 cups	=	0.6 liters
3 cups	=	0.72 liters
3-1/2 cups	=	0.84 liters
4 cups	=	0.96 liters
4-1/2 cups	=	1.08 liters
5 cups	=	1.2 liters
5-1/2 cups	=	1.32 liters

MAIL ORDER SOURCES

Bakers Cash & Carry
367 W. Paxton
Salt Lake City, Utah 84101
(801) 487-3300

Specializing in candymaking and cake decorating supplies and chocolate (retail and wholesale). Everything from candy papers and lollipop sticks, molds, oils, colors and royal icing decorations, to a wide selection of chocolate and 20 colors/flavors of compound coatings. Call or write for mini-catalog. Classes available.

Candy Factory
12510 Magnolia Boulevard
North Hollywood, California 91607
(818) 766-8220

Complete line of candymaking supplies (retail and wholesale). Large selection of chocolate and compound coatings, molds, flavorings, oils, colors, royal icing decorations, cookbooks, etc., and an especially fine assortment of boxes. Classes available.

Country Kitchen
3255 Wells Street
Ft. Wayne, Indiana 46808
(219) 482-4835

All kinds of candymaking and cake decorating supplies. Fine selection of chocolate and compound coatings, molds, lollipop sticks, flavorings, oils, colors, decorations, boxes, thermometers, cookbooks, etc. Catalog available for $3.50; coupon enclosed for $3.50 rebate with orders over $20.00.

Orson H. Gygi Company, Inc.
3500 S. 300 West
Salt Lake City, Utah 84115
(801) 484-6527 or (801) 484-6261

Complete line of candymaking and cake decorating supplies for home and professional use. Large selection of chocolates, tips, colors, virtually every oil-based flavoring available (1-ounce to 1-gallon sizes), lollipop sticks, 22 varieties of lollipop molds, cast aluminum ball molds, plastic molds, thermometers, many etc's.

Haylin's House of Chocolate
8313 27th Street West
Tacoma, Washington 98466
(206) 565-3109

Complete line of candymaking supplies for home and professional use. Extensive selection of chocolates and compound coatings, flavorings, colors, molds, sucker bags and sticks, sanding sugar, filbert paste, boxes, cookbooks, and several products ordinarily available only to commercial candymakers. Catalog is planned.

Kara
University Mall
Orem, UT 84057
(801) 377-5272

Primarily a retail candy shop selling dipping chocolate, basic candy supplies and cookbooks.

Lorraine's
148 Broadway
Hanover, Massachusetts 02339
(617) 826-2877

Complete supply of candymaking and cake decorating equipment—molds, chocolate coating, boxes, bags, thermometers, oils, colors, etc.

Maid of Scandinavia
3244 Raleigh Avenue
Minneapolis, Minnesota 55416
(800) 328-6722

Complete line of candymaking and cake decorating supplies—seemingly anything one could ever want or need. Extensive variety of chocolate, compound coatings, molds, oils, extracts, colors, cookbooks, etc. Catalog available for $1.00.

INDEX

Numbers in *italic* denote photographs   **159**